LaVena Wilkin
Thriving After Workplace Bullying

LaVena Wilkin

Thriving After Workplace Bullying

Journey from Victim to Survivor

DE GRUYTER

ISBN 978-3-11-133212-3
e-ISBN (PDF) 978-3-11-133226-0
e-ISBN (EPUB) 978-3-11-133230-7

Library of Congress Control Number: 2024937628

Bibliographic information published by the Deutsche Nationalbibliothek
The Deutsche Nationalbibliothek lists this publication in the Deutsche Nationalbibliografie;
detailed bibliographic data are available on the Internet at http://dnb.dnb.de.

© 2024 Walter de Gruyter GmbH, Berlin/Boston
Cover design: Hybert Design
Cover image: borisz/iStock/Getty Images Plus
Typesetting: Integra Software Services Pvt. Ltd.
Printing and Binding: CPI books GmbH, Leck

www.degruyter.com

This book is dedicated to the beautiful souls who openly and generously shared their stories with me, even though it occasionally opened up old wounds. These brave and wonderful spirits repeatedly told me they wanted to have their voices heard because it was one step they could take down the path to eliminating workplace bullying and helping other targets. There are excerpts of my conversations with them throughout the book. Out of respect for their privacy, each has been given a pseudonym when mentioned here.

Additionally, I dedicate this book to Bob, my husband and partner in life. Without his help, encouragement, support, and love, I am not sure I would have completed this project. It was a labor of love for me. Bob knows how important it has been for me to tell the stories of the targets and to help others who feel the devastating pain of being bullied. There were times when I was not sure I was doing them justice. He read every word, made suggestions, and held my hand every step of the way. Thank you!

Contents

Introduction

I became interested in the phenomenon of workplace bullying while researching the topic for a class project. I found that many of the studies certainly investigated the causes and effects of workplace bullying, from both an individual and an organizational perspective. However, I was taken aback that so little research had been conducted to help targets of workplace bullying heal from its well-recognized and documented detrimental effects.

My interest in exploring how people cope with the experience of being a target of a workplace bully was heightened when, after learning that my dissertation topic would be workplace bullying, a gentleman asked if I would meet with a friend of his who had been a target of a bully. He hoped I could help her. So, I emailed Anna (not her real name) and scheduled a meeting at a coffee shop near her home. As we talked, it was obvious that her pain, anger, resentment, and blame were raw, and this experience was consuming her life. In fact, her suffering was so fresh that I thought she had recently experienced this emotional trauma; however, I was surprised to hear that it occurred 5 years prior to our meeting. Not only was she still suffering emotionally, but she also had physical ailments that she believed were a direct consequence of her stress from the bullying.

As I drove the 90 miles back home, I could not stop thinking about Anna's story, and it inspired me to explore what it would take for the Annas of the world to begin a healing process. I wondered if other targets of workplace bullying were coping with the aftermath of their experience, and if so, how they learned to cope. This curiosity was the motivation for my research in this area.

This book is based on two grounded theory qualitative research projects (for those of you who care about such things). One project was from my dissertation research and the other from a faculty grant I received to further explore the topic. Data was collected via in-depth semi-structured interviews with people who experienced workplace bullying. I found a clear delineation between targets who were able to cope with the experience and those who are still suffering years after the abuse.

This book tells the stories of targets of workplace bullies, and often those stories paint a picture of downward spirals into depression and disillusionment. Some targets continue to have health problems, suffer emotional distress, and blame the bully and the organizational leaders who ignored the abusive behavior. They are still hurting years later because they do not know how to let it go.

However, the focus of this book is on the resilience of people who had likewise felt wounded, vulnerable, and alone. In their own words, they shared how

https://doi.org/10.1515/9783111332260-001

they were able to move past that hurtful time in their lives. They were able to cope with the bullying when they changed their reactions to the bullying behavior. They were enlightened to recognize they could change neither the bullying behavior nor their leaders' responses to the behavior. They could not change anything external to themselves; the changes came from within. As a result of this realization, they were able to let go of blame and anger and empower themselves to leave the negative and traumatic experiences in the past. They no longer allowed the bully to live rent free in their heads. This is the crux of Enlightened Transformation, the theory that emerged through my research.

To provide a foundation of workplace bullying, I begin with an explanation of this phenomenon, its prevalence, and the behaviors associated with it. I also describe the significant costs and consequences to both the targets and the organizations when bullying is allowed to persist. I will discuss the relationship between power and bullying and how the targets coped with the traumatic experience of being bullied. Ultimately, three interrelated themes emerged from my study. The first is how organizational cultures and norms sanctioned the bullying behavior. A second related theme is that the leaders' lackadaisical responses to reports of bullying influenced how the targets coped with the experiences more than any other factor. The third theme is avoidance. Based on these themes, interviews with targets, and other studies, I offer insights into what targets and organizational leaders can do to deal with bullying behaviors in the workplace. I conclude with a discussion about laws enacted by some countries and how workplace bullying advocates in the United States are advocating for legislation.

Chapter 1
The "So What" of Workplace Bullying

I felt like the walking wounded. I was powerless to change anything. Not only was I broken from within, this workplace I once loved so much was now broken from within. Trust is gone; hope is shattered (Lauren).

While physical violence injures the body, workplace bullying is a type of psychological violence that wounds the minds and souls of targets as they are subjected to ongoing and persistent mental cruelty at the hands of a colleague or their boss (Leymann, 1996). Workplace bullies inflict psychological damage on their targets by subjecting them to ongoing and persistent mental cruelty. They relentlessly belittle, demean, and threaten their co-workers; in addition, targets of workplace bullies often do not let others know what is happening to them.

Prevalence of Workplace Bullying

This epidemic of workplace bullying appears to be contagious. Ruth and Gary Namie, leading authorities on workplace bullying and founders of The Workplace Bullying Institute, commission periodic studies on the prevalence of bullying behavior in the United States. In their 2017 survey, they found that 17% of Americans had been bullied at work. By 2021, this number had almost doubled to 30% (workplacebullying.org). Here are some additional statistics about workplace bullying. These findings are particularly apropos due to the increased number of people working from home after the pandemic:
- Prevalence of bullying has increased 57% since 2017.
- An estimated 48.6 million Americans are bullied at work.
- Bullying during remote work happens mostly in virtual meetings, not via email.
- Remote workers are bullied at a rate of 43.2%.
- Women bully women at twice the rate they bully men.

It is not only the targets who are affected by this negative behavior. An additional 19% of workers have witnessed bullying behavior. People who observe someone being bullied, the bystanders, may begin to think about leaving the organization because they are concerned that they may be the next target.

https://doi.org/10.1515/9783111332260-002

What Is Workplace Bullying?

There is a plethora of terms used to describe workplace bullying, including incivility, bullying, mobbing, workplace aggression, and emotional abuse. For clarity, workplace bullying is the term used throughout this book. However, regardless of the nomenclature, the results are that targets are humiliated, motivation decreases, productivity suffers, and profits decline. The effects are detrimental to both the organization and the individuals.

Stale Einarsen, a foundational researcher of workplace bullying from the University of Bergen, provides a generally accepted definition of workplace bullying. He says it involves behaviors that are hostile or antagonistic. The intent is to provoke, frighten, intimidate, or make the target feel uncomfortable. In order for the label of bullying to be applied to a particular activity, interaction, or process, it has to occur repeatedly and regularly (such as weekly) and over a period of time (such as 6 months). Bullying is an escalating process in the course of which the person confronted ends up in an inferior power position and becomes the target of systematic negative social acts (Einarsen, Zapf, & Cooper, 2003).

Jill, an office manager, said although she had worked in the industry for 25 years, landing a job with this office was her ideal job. Even before she took the job, people warned her about the office bully. Although the organization had trouble keeping employees, she thought, "I can do this. I can handle it. I can make it better. Our positions were equal, so I believe she was threatened by me. She could not just get rid of me, and I was willing to put up with a lot because that was my dream job, and I was not going to give that up easily. There are the people that were confrontational with this person and left their job because of it. There were people that she was able to run off by taking control and complaining about them. But, with me, I don't think she had a way of getting rid of me other than to do it the way she did, which was probably the scariest way. The behaviors started off subtly. For example, she would say hateful things in front of my co-workers. Or she would be behind in her work, so I would offer to help her. She would mock me. When being mean did not make me leave, she escalated her behavior."

The bully's aggressive actions take the form of both verbal and emotional abuse, and they clearly cause humiliation and distress for the target. Although bullying may start as rude or uncivil behavior, if left unchecked, it can escalate into more hostile and antagonistic behaviors. Although the actions represent varying degrees of emotional mistreatment, the outcome is the same: targets are humiliated, and they experience negative emotions of resentment, shame, anger, and grief.

Specifically, workplace bullies use a variety of anti-social and hostile tactics to intimidate their targets. Bullying behaviors lie on a continuum of mild to extreme (Namie, & Namie, 2003). Rayner and Hoel (1997) summed up these bullying behaviors in five categories:

- Threats to Personal Standing
  - Publicly humiliating and ridiculing the target
  - Intimidating the target
  - Spreading rumors and gossip
- Threats to Professional Standing
  - Assigning impossible tasks or workloads
  - Sabotaging the target's work
  - Ostracizing the target
- Isolation
  - Preventing access to professional opportunities, such as training or education
  - Physically or socially isolating the targets from co-workers
  - Intentionally withholding vital information
- Overwork
  - Putting unwarranted demands on the target to produce work
  - Setting impossible deadlines for work completion
  - Continually interrupting work performance
- Destabilization
  - Taking credit for the target's work
  - Assigning superfluous tasks
  - Reminding the target of past work errors

Jill said, "Previously, with other employees, she was the authority figure. We were equals, so she did not have that power over me. However, there was a constant attempt to intimidate me. I loved my job too much to let her run me off, and that turned out to be detrimental to me. One way she would intimidate me by destroying personal things. If I brought a new purse to work, and she didn't like that I had a new purse, suddenly there would be a cut in the purse. No explanation on where that came from, but yet, I knew. She was very clever and very manipulative."

I found a classic example of workplace bullying behaviors in a former academic Dean of a university who was actually the subject of one of my studies. While being investigated for misappropriation of grant money, allegations of intimidation and retaliation surfaced during newspaper interviews with current and former faculty members. Faculty members say the Dean humiliated professors in front of their peers, retaliated against anyone who challenged him, and spread rumors and told lies that were meant to harm them professionally.

Many of the accounts of the Dean's behavior were difficult to believe, yet multiple faculty members told the same stories. In fact, Evan, a participant in one of my studies, said, "If you wrote about it in a novel, people would think well this is interesting, but there is no university anywhere that could operate this way. The real sadness of the story is that this stuff actually happened."

Humiliating faculty in front of their students or colleagues was one tactic this bully used. Cara said she had a class in the computer lab, and unbeknownst to her, the bully had, or he thought he had, reserved the room for him. He stood at the door and blocked her from leaving while he screamed at her in front of the students. This continued for over an hour, and there was a dissertation defense going on in the room next door. She said several students actually wrote to the university leaders and were appalled that the bully treated their professor in this unprofessional manner. In a similar instance, the bully stood outside the door where Josh, the professor, was teaching a class and mocked and ridiculed him in front of his students. The bully told them "You have to help this guy find a new career." He also called all the doctoral students in one night and said that all the faculty was "worthless and that the whole department was worthless."

The bully would also humiliate faculty members in front of their colleagues. Several people talked about the time the Dean called one professor, Allison, out of a faculty meeting. According to Allison, he grabbed her by the shoulders and started screaming, stomping up and down, "shaking me at my shoulders, and telling me that I was an embarrassment to the university." Abby said, "When he pulled Allison out of a public meeting and screamed at her in front of everybody, we couldn't carry on the meeting because we were all just listening to what was going on in the hallway. And it was awful. It was just awful."

Brooke, an administrative assistant in my second study, recalled "One day she started screaming at me in the middle of the office where everyone in the other cubicles could hear her. We were arguing about something that was not something that I had to do. It was not required of me for my job. She started into me. Finally, I was getting nowhere. She was right up in my face. I just finally told her. I told her I was finished talking about it, and I went to my desk. She came over and kept on, and kept on, and kept on. I mean, she had me in tears. People in the office, everybody heard it, everybody. I tried to get a job in a different department. Eventually, they just let me go, and I still don't know why. What I did wrong? I don't know. I really don't know. But it was like this woman was attacking me. It all ended up being my fault. I got fired over it."

Even faculty members who originally supported the Dean quickly fell out of favor with him when they disagreed with him or questioned him. According to Abby, there were originally two people who were finalists for that Dean's position. She said she actually supported hiring this Dean. She was impressed with the ideas he shared during the faculty interview. She thought he would bring much-needed changes to the college. Her opinion started to change during her first meeting with him, when he started mocking the other candidate and saying inappropriate things about other faculty. He made a habit of coming to her office and gossiping about other faculty members. He was pompous and arrogant, and she began to feel uncomfortable around him.

In a faculty meeting after the Dean criticized another faculty member's proposal, Abby said she thought the proposal made a lot of sense. She said, "I was respectful when I spoke up, but I was not going to sit and say nothing because I thought the ideas were good." At that moment, she could feel the shift in the Dean's perception of her. When she countered what the Dean said, she became his enemy. When people saw her coming down the hall, they would "literally duck into their offices"; she realized that people were avoiding her to try to prevent becoming a target themselves. This fear proved to be valid as the one person who was loyal and refused to ostracize Abby became a target of the bully and eventually lost her job.

She said, "I am pretty strong person; I am a confident person; I have been very successful in relationships, as well as in my field. It didn't drown me like it did some of the others, but it still hurt. I just couldn't believe what was happening, and there was no way to stop it."

In my second study, Kameron, an elementary school teacher, provided a similar story of being shunned by her colleagues. She said, "Towards the end of the school year everybody knew what was happening and they were afraid to hang around me. It was guilt by association. So, nobody wanted to be seen with me." It created "us versus them" thinking. She talked further about being isolated from the rest of her colleagues. She said, "He was trying to isolate me from the rest of the faculty. When we had workdays, and the children were not there, and we were supposed to be working on records, he would call up on the intercoms – oh, we are having lunch down here at 11:30, so everybody meet here. They wouldn't call me. So, he was trying to isolate me from them."

Evan said the college had a reputation for having a number of difficult people who were difficult to get along with, and he supported the Dean's ideas. He admitted to falling prey to the Dean's charms. His fall from grace came when a student reported to him that the Dean had sexually harassed her, and he reported that to the administration. Although the report was supposed to be kept confidential, he barely made it back to his office when the Dean called him to his office. He was "yelling, screaming, and red in the face. Literally, you could probably hear him in the next building. He is screaming at me that after everything he has done for me, I am a traitor. At that point, his full blown agenda was to destroy me. My life became hell. Now he has to destroy me and make me out to be completely inept. I went from being able to walk on water and wearing a cape with the big S on it, to not being able to do anything right."

Several faculty members discussed how the bully would call leaders at other universities and tell them not to hire certain people. Evan said that when he interviewed for a position at another university, he told them what was going on. He said to the person interviewing him, "I know this will sound strange, but I feel like if the Dean finds out that I am leaving him and coming here that he will contact you and who knows what he will tell you. So, I am telling you up front. It was interesting that she was a psychologist, and I felt like I was in a therapy session. She was looking at me like you are so close to the situation and emotionally involved. I am sure a Dean would never ever do anything like that. She didn't say it, but just looking at her face . . . she wasn't rolling her eyes exactly.

Then, a couple of weeks later she called and said, 'I owe you a huge apology. He is calling. He called here three times. I refused to talk to him after you and I talked because I knew what was up. However, my assistant comes in to tell me there is a guy on the phone. He is a Dean at the university, and he is demanding to know if Evan is coming to work here. He wants to tell you that Evan is under investigation at the university, and there are a lot of things that you need to know about him.' She said, 'I owe you a big apology. He is doing exactly what you predicted that he might do.'"

Frank told a similar story. He said, "They destroy your confidence. After you were outside the inner circle of trust, they would contact your supervisor if you were trying to get another job and bad mouth you and say that you were only a mediocre professor or employee. They would hit you where it hurts. Basically, they hurt your reputation as far as your work habits or your talent level."

In addition, the Dean prevented people from receiving tenure. Allison explained that when she was up for tenure, the faculty voted that she qualified for tenure. However, the bully set up a separate review committee that changed the rules about the types of journals in which she needed to publish. They denied her tenure based on her research agenda. Likewise, Henry was coming to tenure when the Dean downgraded his annual evaluation from Satisfactory to Unsatisfactory/Needs improvement. With that evaluation, there was no way he could receive tenure. Later, the Dean offered him a 3-year term appointment. He agreed to that because "it is either accept that or another place to go with my tail between my legs. He put me in a position where he had the power. If I got tenure, he couldn't control me. As a term faculty member, he could get rid of me if he needed a tenured position for one of his flunkies."

No doubt, the Dean tormented people he believed were not on his side. This psychological and emotional abuse is not against the law in the United Stated. Other countries, including Sweden, Australia, France, Britain, Finland, Italy, and

Germany, do have laws against workplace bullying. Even though bullying is endemic in American organizations, the United States has lagged behind and has not enacted specific laws that address these negative acts. However, as American companies continue to expand into global markets, they will need to understand and address the problems associated with workplace bullying.

Costs and Consequences of Workplace Bullying

Based on the above descriptions of the bully's treatment of the targets, it is no surprise that targets are less motivated to do their work because they are worried about when the next attack will occur. As a result, job performance suffers. No doubt, people who have been targets of this kind of abuse at work feel demoralized, powerless, and hopeless.

Frank said, "I am a very collegial person. I value faculty involvement, and he was demeaning faculty and constantly haranguing us, telling us how bad we were in his eyes, except for his few golden people who were basically his lapdogs and were doing what he wanted. I have been at the university level for about 35 years, and frankly, I have a lot of love for it. I saw this guy destroying the whole collegial climate of the unit that was part of a major campus. So, I felt a lot of resentment. I felt resentment and I also felt powerless because I had no feeling the higher ups would do anything. Powerless in the sense that I knew they gave him a great deal of power to do what he wanted."

Abby said that being bullied was the most traumatic experience of her life. To put it into perspective, she said that her husband died a few years prior, and while that was a major trauma, it did not compare to being the target of the bully.

In addition, targets report overwhelmingly feeling depressed, irritable, angry, and anxious as a direct result of being bullied (Bjorkqvist, et al., 1994; Quine, 2003). Cara said, "It was awful. I was constantly anxious and constantly nervous. I have never been like that in my life. It was hell." Others spoke about being prescribed anti-depressants just to get through the day. Allison reported going home and crying, and she was not a "crybaby."

Some research indicates that the psychological effects of workplace bullying may linger long after the exposure has stopped, and many victims suffer from symptoms that are consistent with post-traumatic stress disorder (Tehrani, 2004), particularly when they have been exposed to long-term bullying (Einarsen & Mikkelsen, 2003). Victims of Post-Traumatic Stress Disorder (PTSD) experience flashbacks and nightmares, re-live the traumatic event, avoid reminders of the incidents, and suffer intense distress when the event is mentioned (Tehrani, 2004). Post Traumatic Stress

Disorder symptoms can linger 5 years or longer after the exposure has ended (Einarsen & Mikkelsen, 2003).

Beth said, "I started therapy, and when I told my therapist what had happened with the Dean, she said I think you have PTSD". She did PTSD therapy to help her recover. When I met with Jill for our interview, she said, "I had blocked a lot of this out just so I could move forward. When you've experienced it to that extent, it takes such an emotional toll on you."

Additionally, targets of workplace bullying say they experience increased negative physical symptoms, including insomnia, headaches, skin rashes, stomach disorders, and cardiovascular disease (Bjorkqvist, et al., 1994). Thomas (2005) surveyed forty-two support staff employees at a university to determine a relationship between health problems and workplace bullying. Both Allison and Cara were diagnosed with debilitating diseases, one with cancer and one with an autoimmune disease.

Individually, the costs and consequences for the target include:
— Emotional spirals
— Economic loss
— Loss of confidence
— Social isolation
— Stress-related illnesses

As one might imagine, these psychological and physical ailments lead to negative consequences for their organizations, as well. Organizationally, the costs and consequences include:
— Increased absenteeism
— Loss of institutional knowledge
— Loss of productivity
— Loss of reputation
— Turnover
— Presenteeism – being present but not productive.

In most cases, targets are, obviously, less satisfied with their jobs and less motivated to be productive. There is an increased intention to leave the organization. Retention becomes a problem for these organizations, and as skilled workers leave the organizations, they lose a wealth of institutional knowledge. Several participants in my original study mentioned that over forty faculty members left the university as a result of the bullying. Not all were targets. Some were younger faculty members who witnessed what was happening, and they decided they did not want to work for or be associated with an organization that tolerated this behavior toward others.

Targets experience lower organizational commitment to the firm, which has not demonstrated that it provides a psychologically safe work environment. Absenteeism increases due to either medically certified illnesses or the need to take the day off to avoid the bully. Presenteeism is also a factor. Targets may come to work, but they are so focused on avoiding the bully that they are not motivated or productive. Cara explained that she only went to campus when she was teaching a class. If she had to be there any other time, she stayed in her office with the door closed because she wanted to avoid any interaction with the bully. She often missed the collegiality with other faculty members. However, it was more important for her sanity to not risk running into and engaging with the bully.

What does this equate to in profitability? A 2022 study by Kaiser Permanente found that disengaged employees cost companies about 18% of their annual salaries. Likewise, TeamSense reported that the annual cost of employee absenteeism is $225.8 billion, and absenteeism results in about a 40% reduction in productivity (2023). Given these numbers, why would any organization allow bullying to persist? Therein lies the question.

Chapter 2
When Bullies Wear Suits: Don't Let Them Crush You

The bully was like a wild animal, and he was doing what came naturally to him. He attacked people he believed threatened his position or authority, and he did not know any better. However, his keepers (the leaders) knew better, and they did nothing to stop him. (Evan)

Evan's statement illustrates the importance of understanding why adults bully their co-workers and what organizational leaders can do to reduce or eliminate this negative behavior. As I previously discussed in Chapter 1, the bully in my original study was an academic Dean who was in a position of power, and he wielded his power like a destructive sword over faculty members, he did not like or who he felt betrayed him. This is not atypical of workplace bullying. In fact, power is an underlying theme in most bullying cases.

It is estimated that 65% of all workplace bullies are bosses who have power over the targets' daily professional lives (workplacebullying.org). However, having power does not make someone a bully. Rather, bullies abuse their power. Why do adults mistreat their co-workers? What are the attributes of a workplace bully? How does the environment contribute to or encourage bullying behaviors? Knowing these things can help organizational leaders more readily recognize the signs of bullying situations.

Why Do Adults Bully Their Co-workers

For many years, when we thought of bullying, images of the mean kid on the playground taunting and making fun of another child came to mind. Unfortunately, those abusive behaviors have moved from the playground to the office. Since the early 1990s, workplace bullying has been the topic of research studies as scholars attempt to understand why people bully their co-workers. In recent years, some high profile, newsworthy bullying reports have helped the topic gain attention in the popular press. Most studies concluded that there is no definitive cause or reason why people bully or why targets are bullied. In fact, workplace bullying is a social phenomenon with many causes; people bully for a variety of reasons. Most of the time, the explanation is a combination of individual and situational factors.

The very term workplace bully suggests an intertwining of organizational (workplace) and individual (bully) forces. Given the interconnectedness between

https://doi.org/10.1515/9783111332260-003

the organizational and the individual perspective, it is challenging to clearly define the two as there is an interdependent relationship between organizations and individuals; organizations need individuals' skills, creativity, and energy, while individuals need the opportunities, salaries, and careers the organization provides.

Individually, the personality traits of both the target and the bully can contribute to workplace bullying. Targets are often overachievers and perfectionists. They may be viewed as having an idealistic perception of their abilities, resources, and responsibilities. As a result, the bully may perceive the target's tendency to overachieve as patronizing or egotistical, so they retaliate by humiliating the target, withholding vital information, or setting unrealistic expectations for achievement. Bullies may attack the target because they are envious of the target or as an attempt to preserve their own sense of self-worth.

Targets may be bullied because they are different in some way from the rest of the group. They may be quiet in group settings, so they appear to lack social competence or self-confidence. When employees excel at their work and go above and beyond the requirements, the bully may envy the target and feel that the person is a threat to the bully's position or power. Bullies are adept at exploiting their targets' conscientiousness, perfectionism, desire to collaborate, and good temperament (Wilkin & Hymes, 2020). Conversely, bullies may lack social and conflict management skills. They may believe that the target is threatening their self-image, and they are trying to protect their positions in the organization.

In 2019, I had a unique opportunity to write a book chapter with Dr. Bill Hymes (Wilkin & Hymes, 2020). Bill was an accomplished thoracic surgeon who provided an eye-opening view of workplace bullying through a self-admitted bully's lens. We talked specifically about why some people feel the need to humiliate, ridicule, or sabotage their employees or their co-workers. His conversations with me were honest and brutal, and his insights closely align with the recognized reasons adults bully and the attributes of a workplace bully.

Although he believes his story is unremarkable, it provides a profound perspective about workplace bullying through the bully's lens. One reason he believes his story is unremarkable is that workplace bullying occurs so frequently. It is becoming a commonplace occurrence that has become normalized.

When asked about the root causes of workplace bullying, Bill's theory is summed up in three words: pushes, pulls, and permissions.

The pushes (similar to pressure to perform) are:
- Personality – bullies may have a powerful personality that they utilize;
- Personal history – bullies may have a history of success;
- Entitlement – bullies may feel superior, and their strategies justified;
- Personal ambition or quest for status – bullies may be driven to succeed;
- Threats to values or authority – bullies attack any threats.

The pulls (similar to rationalization) are:
- Ease and expedience – may feel that bullying is effective;
- Time pressure and limitation of alternatives – may feel bullying is the only way;
- Past successes – may feel justified due to prior successes;
- Institutional culture – may feel the organizational culture supports the bullying;
- Fear of being taken advantage of – may feel threatened by strong personalities.

The permissions (similar to opportunity) are:
- Power differential – may know that they have power over the targets;
- Insufficient monitoring and control – organizational culture allows the bullying;
- Discounting and deferral of costs – may feel that bullying increases performance.

Bill says that the bully typically works from a deeply held belief of entitlement. He says, "I can tell you that there is not a shred of self-consciousness or doubt. There are convenient excuses forcing one's ideas on others, including time constraints, too many and too varied opinions, and a deeply held belief that one's own point of view is the one true path. It becomes completely natural and reasonable that any disagreement is a threat to outcomes, and thus to the group. Divergent ideas or opinions must be suppressed at all costs" (Wilkin & Hymes, 2020).

Castle's (2014) research focused on the motivations of workplace bullies. Her participants repeatedly told her that they were justified in treating people poorly, and they would do it again if they deemed it necessary. If they did not coerce and threaten people, the job would not have been done correctly. She concluded that people bully because they have an arrogant and self-pretentious point of view. Her research supports Bill Hymes' rationalization for why he was a workplace bully.

The Role of Abusive Power in Workplace Bullying

An underlying theme in most bullying behavior is power, and literature suggests that there needs to be a perceived power imbalance for bullying to occur (Einarsen, 1999; Salin, 2003; Zapf, 1999). To be clear, power in organizations is necessary. Without it, there would be chaos. In his analysis of power, Dahl (1986) argues that power is used to control behaviors or to bring about change, and without power and control, social systems, including organizations, would not function properly or efficiently. Often, destructive power is associated with threatening behavior that can be acted upon when one person has control over something the other person values, for example, economic power over one's money. Additionally, individuals may turn to destructive power when they believe they are losing control or when behaviors are legitimized (Boulding, 1990). Both my studies supported existing research and found that an underlying theme of workplace bullying is abusive power.

Bill said, "I have been a bully. Or put a little more precisely, I have used power in unhealthy ways to achieve my goals and to get others to do what I wanted. It takes less thought, engenders less angst and uncertainty and it cuts out unnecessary discussion. Its attractiveness as a strategy is undeniable, particularly when there is an established pattern of it being used successfully in the past." In fact, he believed that if something was to be done correctly and expediently, bullying behaviors needed to be used to control the process.

Hiring Others to Help Him Bully

Although the Dean initiated much of the bullying, he hired people from the outside and promoted people from within, expecting them to bully their colleagues. Moreover, these positions were filled without input or validation from the faculty. Cara recalled the time when they needed to hire a new department chair. She said, "We voted on whether we wanted to have a search to look for a new chair or whether we wanted to give the job to an internal person. The faculty voted to initiate an outside search. However, the Dean said the faculty voted for the internal candidate. He said the vote was 24–4. I knew that was not the case because I personally knew six people who had voted for an outside search. I went back to them and checked to see if they had indeed voted for an outside search. They had. I actually wrote the Dean an email to let him know that at least six people voted for an outside search. He denied that, and the internal person, one of his lackeys, got the job."

Grady shared a similar story. He said, "I know of one case when the faculty were asked to interview somebody. He was scheduled to show up at 10:00 in the morning, so many of us were there to interview him. We waited around for about half an hour, and he never showed up. We called the Dean's office, and we were told that the person had been offered the job, and the Dean was out showing him neighborhoods for potential housing. We later found out that the chancellor was the only person who met with the guy."

Cara, Ava, Henry, Jack, and Alex discussed how the Dean "wiped out existing leadership and put his own folks in, his own henchmen." They said, "He would bring in people that he knew could write big grants." In order to open up tenure lines for the newly hired people, the Dean either put pressure on people who were not "on his team" to resign, he changed the rules for tenure, or he downgraded evaluations so faculty who were up for tenure were not approved.

Grady said, "The Dean surrounded himself with Associate Deans. I never saw a place with so many Associate Deans and a lot of these positions were created by him to safeguard him and to defend him. He paid astronomical salaries once they were hired as department Chairs or Associate Dean. Big money . . . that would be one factor. Maybe the biggest factor would be that they were in on things. They would be the ones making the decisions. I don't think the rest of the faculty made or were made part of the decision making much at all."

According to Alex, "He sorted through people who would be like him or support him. He was surrounded. Like most dictators he installed a government to support him. We have four departments and four chairs, and none of them were elected by the faculty. The Chair of one department was rejected as unqualified by the search committee, but the Dean bullied the department until they acquiesced to his choice. The Chair of another department falsified her academic credentials. She has no experience as a faculty member. Another person was promoted to the Chair, even though she was rejected by the faculty for this promotion. She is totally unqualified."

The Dean would have "secret leadership team meetings where you were sworn to secrecy, and you could not discuss what happened at the meeting." Evan, who was part of the Dean's inner circle until he fell from grace, talked about things he heard in leadership meetings. He said that each week about fifteen of the Dean's self-chosen chairs, self-chosen Assistant Deans, and self-chosen Deans would meet to "discuss whatever needs to be discussed."

At these meetings, the Dean would openly talk about how this person was out to get him, or how that person was probably stealing grant money, or how another person was lying. "I mean it was just pretty amazing to me that suddenly I am made aware that I am existing in a band of thieves and murderers and serial killers. All of these people who were out to get him were really being regularly assailed in these meetings. And I didn't know any better, I just assumed that this was the status quo, and this is what happens in these circumstances when someone brings in a friendly sheriff to clean things up."

A Flawed Tenure Process

Two stories about the flawed tenure process were shared. In separate interviews, both Abby and Cara discussed the time when Cara was up for tenure. Abby said, "Cara was going up for tenure, and she thought the process was orchestrated to make her fail. I didn't really believe that. In fact, I have always believed that if you do good work you are going to get tenure. Nobody can keep it from you. If you have the publications, you are going to be fine. But it is not true. I saw the worst of the process when I witnessed someone who was on the wrong side in their eyes. She had a dominant personality, and she spoke out against the abuse of power. She had a more brusque manner than I did, so she suffered more. She was enemy #1 of one of the bully's soldiers, Hazel (not her real name). They just didn't see the world in the same way at all. It was a bad relationship from the beginning. And if Hazel didn't like her, the whole team didn't like her.

Hazel got a group of assistant professors together and gave them lines to say in a meeting during Cara's tenure review. These assistant professors in the meeting recited lines of criticism. Literally, one assistant professor who reviewed her case looked at all of her publications, and said, 'I think her research is just local; it is not national.' I actually called him on it. It is the only time I ever did that. But I pointed out that she was going to another state to collect data, and that she is publishing in national journals. He looked straight at Hazel and shrugged as though he was not sure how to respond to that. It was really telling.

The meeting went on, the vote was taken, and she was voted down. It went on to the college level and that is where another member of the posse served on the college-wide committee. Cara's review was mediocre there. It went on to the leadership where it was decided, and Cara did not get tenure. And, she had a good record. She had a better record than some of the Dean's inner circle who were in the same department, and they just sailed through. She thought about fighting it, but it is a really flawed process."

Cara explained this process from her perspective. She said when the faculty voted on her tenure, commented on her research, and they approved her, the vote was unanimous in the areas of teaching, collaboration, ethics, and service. The final vote was 24-0 in each of those areas. In the area of research, the vote was 22-2. Her colleagues were thrilled that she would become tenured. However, Hazel decided that there needed to be a separate review with the personnel committee. This committee voted 5-0, and she met the criteria. Sadly, they voted 2–3 that her research was lacking. As a result, they denied her tenure based on her research agenda.

Likewise, Jack was coming to tenure when the Dean downgraded his annual evaluation from Satisfactory to Unsatisfactory/Needs improvement. With that evaluation, there was no way he could receive tenure. Later, the Dean offered him a 3-year term appointment. He agreed to that because "it is either accept that or another place to go with my tail between my legs. He put me in a position where he had the power. If I got tenure, he couldn't control me. As a term faculty member, he could get rid of me if he needed a tenured position for one of his flunkies." Many participants said one reason people were denied tenure was so that the bully could open up tenure lines for the new faculty he brought in to be part of his team.

These abuses of power were exacerbated by the leaders' failure to deal with the conflict (Strandmark & Hallberg, 2007). The result was that the faculty were divided, camps were created, and trust was shattered.

Grievance? What Grievance?

Many times, the management or financial success of the bully in the eyes of the administration allowed the bully to perpetuate his/her behavior. The culture of the organization stressed achievement over effective management of its people. Consequently, the people suffered, often losing out on promotions or raises, often without recourse.

Evan, who fell from grace when he informed the leaders about a student's report that the Dean had sexually harassed her, tells an incredulous story about the grievance process. He said that after he fell out of favor, the Dean would call him all hours of the day and night, demanding a special report or a project. Every time he would deliver it to the Dean's office, the Dean had his "his goon squad, his inner circle, his Himmler and Goebel" there with him as witnesses. One time, "I walked in and gave him the report. He looks at it, just throws it down and says that is not what I asked for. And he looked at each of them, and said, 'Weren't you there when I called him and told him what I needed.' Of course, they say yes, so he looks at me and says 'Evan, you can't do anything anymore.' It became almost comical how absurd. I just quit doing these things. I told them to fire me. 'If you don't want me in this job anymore, fire me. I am doing a good job, but if you don't want me to do it fine. Just cut the crap of trying to make it sound like I am incompetent. I know too many people. I don't think you are going to successfully convince them that I can no longer walk a straight line and chew gum. If you want to fire me, then just fire me.' But he wouldn't."

Then, when he found out Evan was considering taking another job, he demanded that he resign. Evan said, "he put tremendous pressure on me to resign. Every day I was getting memos and phone calls. It was just nuts. He was just sitting in his office figuring out how he can make my life miserable. Finally, I had to file a grievance to get this stuff to stop. When you file a grievance, all these communications stop.

This is how the grievance process works. There is a judge and a panel of three faculty members. They are the jury. And it is conducted like a courtroom scene. Of course, I have never been involved in that before, but I have been a witness. I knew how to conduct myself. I go first and I present my case. And I have done enough expert witness work to know that when the jury begins nodding their head at me that is a really good sign.

Now it is the Dean's turn to cross examine me and he wasn't very familiar with the process. He asked me a question, then he pounds the table and literally demands that I answer yes or no. I know in court I don't have to do that, so I turned to the judge, and I said 'Your Honor, I have been asked a question and it really does not lend itself to a yes or no answer so I would like to extend it.' I took the next thirty minutes to respond, and he couldn't stop me. He is literally screaming, and the judge is like this man is nuts. He is there screaming for me to shut up that I cannot be saying this stuff. It was the most bizarre situation.

I did not hire my own attorney because the only thing that person can do is provide advice. I was not going to spend a whole lot of money to have an attorney sitting there with me. I was asking him to get off my back about resigning. I wanted him to quit contacting my potential future employer. I wanted him to stop pulling the shenanigans with my salary. Just cease and desist. The university hired a counsel for him.

Then, we took a break, and during the break, his counsel comes to me, and she says the Dean knows he is going to lose this grievance. He is prepared to give you what you want in your settlement here. All you have to do is stop the grievance. In other words, you say you stop the grievance, and we give you all of the stuff that you are grieving for. And in turn, it is sealed and the disposition that you stopped the process.

I asked her why I would want to do that, since I knew I would win the grievance. She was very arrogant. And, she had reason to be. She said, 'Evan, you know you can get what you want, which is why we are doing this grievance process, or you can move forward with the grievance. And if you win the grievance you need to know that the outcome of the grievance is simply advisory to the administration. And we both know where the administration stands on all of this. In other words, you can win the grievance and it goes to the administration. The administration throws it in the garbage, and the Dean continues to do whatever it is that you claim he is doing.

If you look at it that way and you know that she is telling the absolute truth, because I had gone to the administration, and I became aware very, very quickly that when I went to them about these issues, I was told, and this is beautiful, this is just so beautiful, go work it out with the Dean. Imagine that a criminal is beating you with a baseball bat, and you run to a police officer who says you need to go and work it out with the criminal. I was being told you can win the grievance; you can win the battle and lose the war. Or you can get what you want and get him off your back by signing a confidential agreement, and you just go off into the sunset whenever you are ready and that is all there is to it. So, I stopped the grievance. All the grievances that were filed against him were ended I am sure in exactly the same way, so there was not a record of any grievances."

According to Grady, 30 grievances were filed. However, many faculty said that the grievance process was the reason the complaints and allegations of bullying behavior against the Dean were never formalized. Grievances were either dismissed or a deal was made, so written reprimands were not part of permanent records. Indeed, nine of the ten faculty members who participated in my study filed grievances.

Abby said, "the grievance officer went over to administration multiple times and told them this is not one person who is reporting this behavior. This is not a small group of people. This is systemic. In fact, 50% of the faculty would have been to see her that year." Abby said that she filed a grievance, but she did not win. Originally, she wanted to name both the Dean and the department chair, but she only named the Dean. She thought if they teamed up, they would be formidable. She did not hire counsel because she was told by the faculty grievance officer that this is a collegial process. Everyone is supposed to act professionally and get along. The university did have their attorneys there. She said they attacked her character and denied any wrongdoing. Then, after the grievance, everything got worse.

In her own words, "He is like a pit bulldog. Once he gets a hold of you, he never would let go. It became known that if you filed grievance against the Dean or any of his chief lieutenants, there would be hell to pay and retribution. Also, the word was out that the grievance process was not friendly toward faculty, not fair toward faculty, and you were likely to come out with absolutely nothing but hell to pay."

The Ultimate Abuse of Power

The Dean displayed an ultimate abuse of power when it became public knowledge that he misappropriated federal grant money, and he was arrested. Eventually, he pleaded guilty to the crime and received a prison sentence. Many of the participants stated he was "not tried for his real crimes." Abby said, "you know the whole criminal case of the stealing of millions of dollars is the reason any of the bullying came to light. It is the reason you are doing this study. Nobody would know this, and that is very sad that it took the guy stealing money for him to get in trouble. The bullying was not important until it had to do with money."

Jack lamented, "the fact of the matter is that he is not tried for his real crimes. The damage that he did to human lives, careers, people's emotional stability, their mental health, and their physical health brought on by the duress . . . . . .

those were his real crimes, more important crimes. This is just something he did for money. Far less important." Likewise, Evan said, "And probably the least egregious thing that he did was steal millions of dollars."

Attributes of the Bully

Participants in my original study described the bully as a person who was charismatic and seductive when you were one of his chosen team. He called those who were not part of his inner circle the "losership team." In addition, he could turn manipulative, vindictive, paranoid, and narcissistic if he believed you had betrayed him, or if you questioned him or his motives. He was a psychologist who knew how to persuade and manipulate people.

Evan said the Dean was "flawed" and "ill." He said, "By the time he was leaving he was making over $250,000, and he was doing consulting everywhere. He had all the money he needed. He is the Dean of a large college within a university system; he has prestige; he has power; he has financial resources. It would seem that he has everything he needs to be happy. All he had to do was take his own innate abilities as a very bright, creative, and accomplished individual and simply apply them even at 50%. He would have been remarkably successful. There is something inside of him that won't let him operate within society in a way that he ought to. And people with flawed personalities in a university are just horrible to deal with."

Jack said, "He could talk the birds out of the trees. When the leaders asked him about the reports of bullying, it is just quite possible that he presented himself as a suffering party. He was just trying to get maximized productivity in the college and these people are ganging up on him." He went on to say, "He is such a manipulator of people's minds. He knows how to push your buttons and get a result. He knows what to say to get you on board."

Grady noted that, "After he was there for a couple of months I could tell he ruled out of fear, and he attempted to motivate people in a very negative, fearful fashion. I also thought some of his actions were very narcissistic, kind of borderline personality, so my coping mechanism was to avoid him as much as possible. When I was in meetings with him he would publicly criticize everything I was interested in or any suggestions I had. He would tell me my ideas were worthless. However, I saw him bully other people even more than he did me. One day I saw him outside of my office really riding out a young professor. I didn't know what the particular topic was, but I came out in the hallway, and I told him to leave her alone or something of that effect. And I told that professor that if she ever needed any eyewitness account of what happened I would be glad to be such a witness. That young professor he was berating later went on leave for a fairly long time hoping the dean would leave before she came up for tenure. I tended to avoid the guy after seeing him in action. I thought he either had deep psychological problems or he was just a moral monster."

In my second study, Jill said of a bullying woman in her office, "I think this person (the bully) had issues. She was on medication. My colleagues saw what was happening, and they would sympathize. They told me if she got her medications straightened out, she would be better. I hoped for that. But then, there were drinking issues, too. She was clever and manipulative." She went on to say, "her personality would switch at times. I think that's part of the bullying. They become this nice person that you think, 'They're nice today.' This is the person that I would like to work with. Then, if something in her personal life isn't going right, she would lash out and be angry again. It's this roller coaster of emotions that you deal with because of their illness. You don't know which personality is going to show up for work that day. Will it be the nice person you can work with? Or the one that you can't turn your back on because you don't know what's going to happen?"

Some ways the targets in my original study described the bully are:
- Is pompous and arrogant;
- Is a Sociopath/Narcissistic/Machiavellian;
- Is a manipulator of people's minds;
- Knows how to push your buttons;
- Does not trust anyone/believes sooner or later you will betray him;
- Could be very charismatic/knows what to offer to get you on his side;
- Has deep psychological problems;
- Is a moral monster.

These characteristics are consistent with research that posits bullies have an inexplicable ability to manipulate people and abuse their power. In addition, bullies typically work from a deeply held belief of entitlement, and they look for and exploit the targets' vulnerabilities. In my original study, the vulnerabilities were not weak personalities or incompetent individuals. Most faculty members had earned doctorates, had published in scholarly journals, and were intelligent, articulate, and respected by their peers. Several also confronted the bully and reported the behavior to the university leaders. Therefore, their exploited vulnerabilities could be identified as feeling deceived and disillusioned and experiencing hopelessness and powerlessness with the situation because the administration ignored or dismissed their reports of the bullying behavior. I will explore these concepts further in the next section.

How Targets Experienced the Bullying

As I mentioned above, while some initially felt deceived and disillusioned by both the bully and the organizational leaders, others initially experienced deeper feelings of powerlessness and hopelessness. Moreover, it was common for targets who initially just felt disillusioned to have that spiral into feelings of being hopeless and powerless; no one was listening to or validating their reports of being bullied. Therefore, at first, they felt just disillusionment, but it advanced to more serious feelings of despair and hopelessness as the bullying behaviors progressed.

Feeling Deceived and Disillusioned

In the beginning, although they were bewildered by his behavior, some professors shrugged it off, thinking he would change his behavior after he got to know the faculty better. Henry would tell people, "Give the guy a break he is really just trying to make changes, and some people are not on board because they are afraid of change." Conversely, those new to the college accepted what he said because they did not know the faculty well enough.

In fact, faculty participants reported that they were initially impressed with his interview, and even voted for him over the internal candidate for the Dean's position. Abby said, "About half of the faculty wanted the interim Dean, and about half wanted this Dean, who was an outside candidate. And I actually wanted the outside candidate. At the interview, he gave a talk that at the time I thought was somewhat impressive. I thought at the time that he would bring needed change. The interim Dean was nice, but I was concerned that he would not be able to move us forward in the direction we needed to go."

During the interview, the Dean expressed the desire for transparency and keeping people apprised of the changes that would be implemented. Then, almost immediately after he was hired, he began to hold private leadership meetings, and the members of the leadership team were sworn to secrecy. Cara noted that "one of the Dean's key words was that he was going to make things transparent. And we had a little joke among some of us where we would say we should write on an overhead transparency 'are things transparent yet?' We joked that we should tape the word 'transparency' up on the walls and doors around the college. He kept saying he was trying to make them transparent, and he was obviously making them very opaque." Participants who were once a part of this chosen group reported becoming disillusioned when the Dean would openly mock and criticize professors in the meetings.

Feeling Hopeless and Powerless

When targets believe that their reports of bullying behavior will not be addressed, they may experience feelings of hopelessness and powerlessness (LaVan & Martin, 2008; Strandmark & Hallberg, 2007). My original study confirms both of those previous studies. Faculty reported their feelings of deception and disillusionment spiraled into deeper emotions of hopelessness and powerlessness when their voices were not heard by the university leaders. Henry said, "That is the most frustrating part of this. You remain with your hands tied. You remain helpless. The system is not working."

Abby said, "They tried to damage my reputation, and it really worked. It was just heartbreaking. There were times when I would just go home and cry. I am not even a crybaby or anything. I have this incredible life with all of these great things happening, and I just felt helpless. All of this stuff was happening to me and being said about me that I couldn't control. I didn't understand and I didn't know how people could hate so much. I actually think a lot of the hate was from the department chair, rather than from the Dean. He was an obnoxious person who did not forgive if you were not on his side. It was the ganging up on me, the team effort to destroy me, that demoralized me. It wasn't that I couldn't handle the Dean. He was aggressive and in your face yelling, where the department chair did it all behind my back." Grady said, "I felt resentment and I also felt powerless in the sense of again I had no feeling the administration would do anything. I felt powerless in the sense that I knew they gave him a great deal of power to do what he wanted." She could not fight the system that was broken from within.

Chapter 3
The Leader's Role in Workplace Bullying: Crack Down on It or Support It

It is anonymous crap. The Dean is doing a good job. (College Administrator)

An organization's leaders can either intentionally or unintentionally support and promote a culture of workplace bullying. Interestingly, some participants see the bullying as a symptom of an organizational culture that legitimized the bullying. One noteworthy finding of my research was that the targets were angrier and more frustrated with the administrators than they were with the bully. Ava and Alex believed they were complicit because they knew what was happening, and they did not stop it. Ava, Jack, Alex, and Abby said the administrators were incompetent because they had the power to stop the hostile behavior, and they did not put an end to it. Overwhelmingly, they felt as though the administrators not only allowed the bullying to exist but also to thrive.

Grady confirmed that with his thoughts. He said, "I have resentment against the sacrosanct who were just able to do whatever they wanted and got rewarded for it. No one gave a damn about the other faculty. I resent administrators who did nothing. And I feel bad for the faculty, staff, and students. It also affected a number of doctoral students who I still communicate with, and every time I mention his name, they have such hatred for the guy.

I feel anger resentment and a feeling of sadness about the lives of both faculty and students. When twenty-one faculty quit, there are about thirty grievances against him, and there were at least two sexual harassment charges against him, how in the world could the administration did not see this? How could they not do anything? I am incredulous about how unbelievably crazy, negligent, and neglectful they were. I have anger not just towards him but also toward the upper administration. Again, the university has been my life for so long I feel resentment toward anyone for anyone who would corrupt a university.

I am glad I left. I am glad I am not there any longer. However, that town was one of the best places I have ever lived. I might have stayed there the rest of my career had we not had this monstrous Dean. I think they are slowly pulling themselves together from what I hear. But those lives they cannot compensate those people enough for what was done."

During a live news telecast, a reporter asked an administrator about faculty allegations that they were being mistreated at the hands of the Dean. The administrator angrily responded that the reports were "anonymous crap." To be fair,

https://doi.org/10.1515/9783111332260-004

some people did send anonymous messages to the administration because they were afraid of retribution.

However, a letter signed by 21 faculty members documented that many faculty reported the behavior to the administration. Ava believed that "this is true reflection of the administration." Organizational leaders who reward bullying by promoting or praising the bullies and denying that bullying is a problem, promote, support, and legitimize bullying behavior (Hoel & Cooper, 2001).

Over and over, the bully openly boasted that he had the full support of the administration. Abby said, "Early on the Dean got wind that people did not like him. At every meeting, he would say 'I have the full support of the administrators.' He was a fast talker, and sometimes he would repeat himself three or four times. It was as though that was his mantra. And, he did have the full support of them from early on really to the final hour. Even after his office was raided by the FBI and he was arrested, one administrator sent him an email telling him how much he would be missed." Jack noted that the Dean literally bragged in faculty meetings that the administration was his ally and "he could do whatever he wanted because the administrators would support him no matter what."

His mantra was supported when the faculty reported the behavior to the diversity officer, human resources, and high-level administrators, and no action was taken to stop the bullying. Over and over, targets said, "no one was listening" and "we had nowhere to go for help." Alex likened it to "a family where the older boys are beating up on the younger siblings. When the siblings go to the parents, not only do they ignore it, but they tell them to handle it themselves. They hand the bully the whip. The administrator was more interested in politics and advancing the university to a high-level research institution. So, even though the behavior was reported to the administrators, no action was taken. They protected the bully, and they said there was no proof of wrongdoing. The administrators need to resign. And all of the Dean's henchmen should have been removed earlier. They just came out unscathed. That is the story behind the story of how he got away with this. It is really their personal failure." When leaders dismiss or ignore reports of bullying, they intensify the problem and contribute to the pervasiveness of the behaviors (Georgakopoulos, Kent, & Wilkin, 2011).

When asked why the administrators did not stop the bullying, Cara said, "Since they did not do anything about the reports, it seems as though they chose to participate. What could possibly be their reason for not stopping the hostile behavior? It is true that the Dean was really crafty. Even I thought he was there to make changes, and when you make changes, you make people angry. People in the community commented to the administration that there is something wrong in this college, and the administration would respond that they were just cleaning house. That is bound to make some people angry." When organizational leaders accept bullying behavior or excuse it as part of the change process, it not only persists but also intensifies (Ashforth, 1999; Crawford, 1999).

A Word About Change

Change can be a factor that increases opportunities for workplace conflicts, including bullying. In fact, changing key management positions (Baron & Neuman, 1998) and other organizational changes (Skogstad et al., 2007) are predictors of bullying behavior. Sometimes, bullying behaviors may be ignored, tolerated, or misinterpreted by the administrators as a deliberate strategy, especially when organizational changes are being implemented. The results of my study supported that contention. The bullying began when the Dean was hired to change the university to a top-tiered research institution. In part, the bullying and abuses of power were tolerated and accepted because the Dean had a reputation for securing federal grant money that would be needed to achieve this designation.

The administrators had their eyes on the prize of becoming a top-tiered research institution. In some cases, the targets felt as though the laser focused on the ultimate outcome, which resulted in the end justifying the means. Receiving federal grant money was one way they could accomplish the goal, and the Dean had a reputation for bringing in grants. Since that goal was so important to them, whatever it took to get there was acceptable.

In addition to the administrators, some of the faculty members who eventually became the Dean's targets also initially thought that he would be the one who could make the needed changes in the college. Evan mentioned that the college had a reputation for having a number of people who were difficult to get along with. He said that the Dean who was there before the bully "was a very nice guy who cared about the college and the faculty. I heard that the faculty ran him off, and I assumed this is what happens when a friendly sheriff is brought in to clean things up." Other faculty agreed that the college was dysfunctional, it lacked strong leadership, and it needed to change. However, the administrators' objective of changing the college seems to have degraded into the Dean's ambition for power and personal advancement, which meant rewarding his cronies and punishing his detractors.

Leaders' Role: Through The Eyes of a Bully

Bill, the surgeon who had been both a bully and a target, noted that sometimes it is difficult to distinguish between apathy about abuse and poor leadership. In fact, even when the abuse becomes obvious, leaders are tempted to deny the problem and avoid any discussions about the behaviors. Many leaders have no training on how to engage in constructive conversations or conflict management. It is easier to simply ignore the behaviors. He goes on to say that leaders are often ill-prepared to lead, and it is easy to fall prey to the illusion that we are much better leaders in our minds than in reality (Wilkin and Hymes, 2020).

In addition, leaders can dismiss allegations of workplace bullying, believing it is just tough management. Sometimes, the continuum of behaviors blurs that line between the two. Daniel's (2009) research determined that the overarching factor that sets workplace bullying apart from tough managers is the bully acts with malice, and the tough manager values humanity. Below is a comparison of a tough manager and a workplace bully (Daniel, 2009) (Table 1).

Table 1: Comparison of workplace bullies and tough managers.

Workplace Bullies	Tough Managers
Abuse of power	Objective and fair
Personally focused	Organizationally focused
Emotional outbursts	Unemotional
Unfair/inconsistent actions	Objective

From Bill's perspective, a tough manager enforces standards that help the organization achieve productivity and profitability. They may be tough, but they are objective, fair, and consistent in their treatment of all employees.

Perception: There Was a Complete Lack of Respect

Consistently, the faculty members told me they did not feel valued or respected by the administration. In addition to the leaders dismissing their allegations and perverting the grievance procedures, they discussed how the report from the consulting firm was not shared, and that there was a huge amount of turnover in that particular college.

The faculty also divulged to me one additional especially important failing of the leadership – faculty governance was ignored. In many universities (including the one in my study), the faculty is required to be in control of many aspects of the educational processes. This requirement is normally imposed by the school's accrediting agency and meeting that requirement is extremely important. The faculty should set the curriculum and also have input into the hiring decisions of their department. In my study, the faculty had no say in who was being hired; the Dean brought in people who supported his agenda. In addition, the faculty had a vote of no confidence in the Dean; this vote was totally ignored by the administration.

Ignoring Faculty Governance

Several professors provided examples of how the Dean ignored faculty governance. Cara said, "Remember, universities are run by faculty governance, and the faculty governance and the faculty senate were totally disregarded. When a faculty member receives a grant, a percentage would go to the department, and the department could decide how to spend it. Toward the end of the year, the department Chair, one of the Dean's lackeys, came to the meeting and said that the funding was not going to come to the department that way anymore. All of the money was going to go straight to the Dean's office, and then he would dole it out based on the need in the different departments. I protested and said that was not fair. I asked her if we really wanted to vote to do that. She said, 'you don't get to vote to do it; the Dean is the Dean, and he is going to do it that way.' I argued for 30 minutes; I got the bylaws out; and in the end, when the Dean decided to change the rules, the faculty had no voice in the matter."

Evan, Cara, Ava, Henry, Lily, and Grady all discussed how the faculty had a vote of "no confidence" against the Dean. It took a lot of courage for faculty to vote against him because it was an open vote, and if a faculty member who did not have tenure voted against him, he would likely fire them on the spot.

Evan said, "Here you have a situation that is similar to a scene from 'On The Waterfront,' the old Marlon Brando movie. Basically, they are trying to organize the union on the waterfront, and it takes courage for union workers to step up knowing that there are a bunch of goons hanging around with baseball bats, trying to beat them out of trying to form a union. You can imagine having a faculty meeting that the Dean is conducting and there is a vote on the floor of no confidence. That vote is going to be public knowledge. The Dean is going to know how you voted, and you had better believe that if you are a non-tenured faculty member, he will get rid of you on the spot. And for that vote to go through, under those circumstances with him in the room literally counting votes is so powerful. In most meetings, he would literally get in your face if you disagreed or contradicted him. The fact that the 'no confidence' vote went through is phenomenal."

Unfortunately, even though the document was taken directly to the President's office by one of the faculty members, nothing was done. The administrators admitted there were a few problems, but they were told to work it out with the Dean. The vote was disregarded.

Henry said, "the system failed due to lack of consideration of faculty governance. And this is so distracting to people who are trying to do their work. You have to engage in self-defense. You lose your focus, and in fact they do win. They destroy you because then you are not as productive. Once you become the target of institutional bullying, you can kiss it goodbye, you are going to have to try and leave."

Finally, Our Someone is Listening . . . Not

As a result of the vote of no confidence in the Dean, the administration hired a mediation consulting firm to look into the problems. The faculty thought, "finally someone is listening." Evan said, "They brought in a consulting firm to study the issues. However, the results were never known. They were never shared with any of us. I am sure they realized withing five seconds 'my God, you have huge problems.' The faculty wanted to know what they found, but the administration buried the report."

Abby tells a similar story. She said, "my colleague and I went to the administration to talk about some issues, and they finally listened to us. The administration said they knew about an organization that had a reputation for working miracles when there is conflict in the workplace. They decided to hire them, and we would schedule time to talk to them in groups. The administration assured us everything would be ironed out. We were so excited and so naïve. We thought things would begin to change.

The administration gave that group several names of people to speak with, and consultants met with several of us. I had an opportunity to look at the list of people. Both my colleague and I were on the list. However, so were the Dean and several of his henchmen. All of the people he had given these huge raises and constant accolades for their work. While a bit discouraged, I thought the consultants were quite skilled. I was really impressed with the questions they asked. They were trying to understand and dig deep.

After they finished interviewing us, we waited and waited for the report. While we are waiting, the Dean does more stuff. He is screaming at people, and there are more embarrassing and humiliating situations. It was awful. Eventually, some of us wrote to the administration and asked to see the report. The administration said there was not a report.

Eventually, we received a one-page letter co-written by the Dean and the administration. The message was to just get back to work and stop complaining. It was the most demoralizing period of the whole thing for all of us. We were so utterly let down because we knew it was a fight to get our voices heard. We had been trying and trying. We had hope for a few minutes. Now that hope was demolished. I knew at that time that nothing was ever going to change."

High Levels of Turnover

Finally, the belief that the organizational culture did not value faculty was bolstered by the number of faculty who left the university as a result of either being bullied or witnessing bullying behavior toward others. Abby's sentiment that nothing was going to change was echoed by every participant in my study. In fact, in response to the administration's claim that the allegations were "anonymous crap," twenty-one faculty members signed a letter to the board of trustees documenting that they had indeed attempted to follow proper procedures by first going to the Dean and then reporting the behaviors to the administration.

Evan said, "The Dean ran a lot of people off who either retired early or took other jobs. We got twenty-one people to sign that letter, but there were a lot more who could have signed. It was August, classes were not in session, and we did not know how to contact them. We could have had forty signatures on the letter."

There were other faculty who left the university without signing the letter because they simply wanted to move on with their lives. Abby said, "Some of the biggest victims did not sign the letter. One was publicly humiliated by the Dean. One was the target of Pricilla, one of the Dean's flunkies. There were several others who were severe targets, but they just wanted to put it all behind them. They did not want to be associated with the mess." Henry said, "people refused to sign the letter because they were afraid it would ruin their careers. That is what the bully does. He destroys your confidence." Also, they did not ask anyone to sign who was still employed at the university.

Reactions to the Bullying Behavior

The participants in my original study were strong, intelligent, articulate, self-confident individuals with earned doctorates. Many were well-known in their individual areas of expertise. They had written books, were published in scholarly journals, and consulted and collaborated with other experts. They were not weak, shy, or introverted. As a result, when the bullying occurred, all but two of the ten participants in the original study confronted him in an attempt to resolve the problem. When that did not work, they personally met with or wrote to the administrators. Incredibly, more than one-third of the full-time faculty in the college reported the behaviors to the faculty grievance officer. Eventually, the grievance office resigned.

Evan tells about one time when he was fed up with the Dean screaming at him. He said, "I am tenured, and I finally had it. I told him to sit down and calm down. The Dean always made a big deal about growing up in New York city in hard times, and he thought of himself as a hardened street guy. 'Calm down,' I said. I told him he would not last fifteen minutes in my neighborhood. He was not intimidating me. It was funny to watch him go from red-faced and pounding on the table to shifting gears and acting like a victim.

When he realized that he could not intimidate me, he used the Russian mafia approach. He killed my family. When I took the position, he authorized bringing on new faculty and buying new equipment. He started to renege on those promises. He got rid of graduate assistantships. He fired my new faculty. That was difficult to watch because they had not done anything wrong."

As a result of the administration's refusal to acknowledge that the Dean's behavior was harming the faculty, many of them felt powerless to change the situation. Grace and Lily chose not to confront the Dean because they believed he was emotionally unstable and they did not know how he would react; they both eventually left the university, which is an avoiding strategy. Others who were initially confronted eventually left the university, worked from home, or took sabbaticals. Ultimately, all ten participants eventually chose some form of avoidance behavior as a way to deal with the bullying experience. Part of that avoidance resulted from a lack of trust. The bullying behavior destroyed the sense of collegiality among the faculty. Ava said, "Faculty were fearful. They did not know who they could trust, so they just stayed in their offices. The collegiality we once shared was gone. He divided people. There were camps."

Overall, more than forty faculty members left during the years the Dean was there. Even people who were not bullied left because they saw how the Dean acted and realized that the administrators discounted accounts of the bullying and failed to deal productively with the behavior. They did not want to be associated with a university that had so little respect for the faculty, so they cut their losses and found other jobs.

Consequences of the Coping Strategies

These confronting and avoiding strategies had consequences, both positive and negative, for the faculty. The consequences were:
- Separation – many left not only the university but also lost family and friends as well
- Productivity – many accomplished more as they stayed away from the university

- Vulnerability – many suffered financially, acquired health problems, or lost all trust
- Acceptance – some just accepted the situation and tied to avoid the Dean
- Validation – some found articles that validated what was happening to them

Many of the faculty avoided the Dean and the administration by leaving the university. They discussed separations from their husbands, wives, and friends. One professor ended up divorcing and leaving a home she loved. One left her husband behind when she took a job in another state. Even though he eventually joined her, she talked about missing friends, family, and grandchildren in her home state. Also, remember that Grady said he would likely have stayed there the rest of his career because he loved the city so much.

Abby said, "That city had been my home for years. My husband and I raised a family, we have grandchildren, and we built an entire life in the city. I still consider it my home, and I never thought I would leave. I love, loved (I do not anymore) the University. I am a big basketball fan, and we have season tickets and great seats. Somewhere along the way, the switch tripped for me, and I just thought I am going to do my own work I am going to quit fighting. I would stay home a lot. You know I still taught my classes; I loved teaching there. The students are so phenomenal. I love the whole urban area of the city.

I knew I was marketable, and I could get a job. I came to this university for a job interview, and it was perfect. I have never felt such a burden lifted in my life. It was so freeing. I eventually wrote a one-sentence email to the Dean, and said I was leaving. After all of the horrible things he has said and done to me he comes running into my office and says, 'You know I do not want you to go.' He acknowledged that horrible things happened, but he did not want me to leave."

Henry said, "He isolated me. Here is a good example. He actually had one of his goons separate me from my department. After I challenged him, his goon came to my office and told me he was replacing me as the department Chair because I was no longer trustworthy. He said that I should really consider working some other place because I was not going to thrive there any longer. The climate here is not working for you. Basically, he was telling me I was going to be forced to do what he told me to do. I knew then when he took away my meritorious rating that he would not give me a raise.

That is when I reprimanded the guy, and I showed him the door. I told him to get out of my office and that he had gone too far in trying to pressure me. At that time, I already knew I had a job someplace else. But imagine if I didn't."

Cara discussed being separated from committee work that she loved. She said, "I served on several committees, and I loved that work. We were revising policies and making much needed changes. I was the leader on one of the committees, and all of a sudden, the committee was disbanded, and it was being restructured. I was not invited to participate on the new committee."

People also mentioned being separated from friends during this time because unless someone has been a target of bullying, it is difficult for them to comprehend the depths of the destructive behavior. Jack said, "the fact of the matter is some of your friendships suffer because every day you are telling them about what this no-good Rasputin sociopath has done to you or to somebody else. You get the feeling that they are just thinking you are complaining. After all of this became public knowledge in the newspaper, my close friends and associates said, 'now we know what you were talking about.' Otherwise, unless it becomes public you are viewed as a complainer."

Productivity was a positive consequence of avoiding the Dean. Abby also said during the time when she was exposed to the bullying, she would stay home and work on her research and writing every chance she got. She had eight major publications in a year. She took a sabbatical, wrote a book, and learned to speak a foreign language. She developed a healthier lifestyle and lost some weight. She was happy and productive until she came back to work and realized that the environment was still toxic.

Another unfortunate consequence of avoidance was vulnerability. Ava took unpaid time away from the university, and she borrowed from her retirement fund to live. She said, "I just tried to do things that I enjoyed. It was good to be away, and I don't think I could have stood it one more minute. But there was such a toll on me financially, so I worried about that a lot. And we have loans from this time that I took off."

Grace ended up selling her house and moving in with her family. Both became financially vulnerable. For others, vulnerability took the shape of stress-related illnesses. Ava also feels vulnerable because if this happened once, it could happen again. She said, "I still do not like to be in my workplace. I am uncomfortable. Sometimes I just have to get up and leave. I do not trust people in my workplace like I did in the past. The Dean maybe be gone now, but the administration is the same. I feel like I am vulnerable. I do not trust what the next thing may be or how they will handle it. I used to enjoy my work, but now I do not. I feel dramatically different about it."

Additionally, acceptance was another consequence of avoidance. Alex said, "All of us who tried to enact changes were soundly put down and put into our places, so the best coping strategy is to avoid. There was no available coping except avoidance. Stay away from the college." Grady made similar statements. He said, "I chose to avoid the bully because I accepted that the administrators would not intervene. A guy like him could go sort of uncocked. You have no idea what he would do, so my strategy was to stay away from him as much as possible and try to ignore him as much as possible. After a few months, I had a feeling he was either a nut or entirely unethical. He would have the sanction of the higher ups in doing whatever he wanted so he had almost a kind of free reign. So, you know the old aphorism 'absolute power corrupts absolutely.'"

The final consequence I identified that resulted from avoiding was validation. In addition to the validation of being employed by other universities that respected their abilities and treated them well, the faculty found validation in an article in the Chronicle of Higher Education that named the behaviors as workplace bullying. Abby said when she read it, she made copies and gave them to her colleagues. "I copied it, and I gave it to people. It was so helpful because we knew it helped us have a name for what was happening to us." Lily said, "it is time for a study to be published on something like this. This is not a unique thing. It has happened in other places, and it tells you human nature has an ugly side to it. It is nice that there is somebody from the outside that sees this. Thank you for wanting to make a difference because we are kind of broken from within." Abby concurred. She said, "I think you are going to have a phenomenal piece on your hands. I hope it can get into some of the major publications, and I hope it gets the word out there."

Likewise, Jill said, "I think it's such an important topic. Thank you for caring enough to hear stories from people like me who have experienced this. For somebody like me, that is such a blessing. I am so grateful to be sitting here on this sofa telling my story. You listened intently and let me experience my emotions, and I thought I had dealt with those emotions. That is such a healing thing for people like me to go through. I can't thank you enough for allowing me to share my story. Hopefully, what I went through will not be in vain if I can help others. I want to thank you. I'm so grateful for this research that you're doing."

Simply listening to the stories of people who had been targeted by a workplace bully validated them. This was especially true for targets whose leaders refused to listen.

The participants who described themselves as self-confident, articulate, intelligent professionals shared their stories about having their self-confidence undermined, feeling demoralized, and feeling professionally inept. The primary reason for their conflicted self-perceptions was that the university leaders discounted their accounts of being bullied and refused to stop the bullying behavior. While they knew the treatment was unjust, the administrators' refusal to deal with it gave the bully absolute power. Their reaction validated and legitimized the bully's behavior, and devalued and disregarded the faculty's concerns. In order to move forward and cope with the experience of being bullied, the faculty needed confirmation that their concerns were valid.

Chapter 4
The Role of Resilience: Broken but Repairable

Resilience is a huge part of how we just keep moving. It is how we move forward through any adversity. Hailey

Individuals who appeared to being better able to cope with the experience of being a target of a workplace bully specifically mentioned resilience. Psychologists define resilience as a person's ability to adjust and function competently even when they are exposed to adversity, experience trauma, or are in a high-risk group. Not only do they find the inner strength to survive, but these distressing experiences may also lead to personal development (Garmezy, 1991). The adversity is not denied, nor is it dismissed. Resilient individuals feel the pain and trauma of the bullying behavior. They ride on the emotional roller coaster of feeling angry, frustrated, hopeless, and disillusioned.

However, the experience of being a target did not define who they are as individuals. They did not allow the bully to live rent free in their heads.

Factors that influence an individual's resiliency are:
- Positive attitude about life
- Cohesive family relationships
- External support systems, including strong friendships and spiritual connections
- Internal locus of control (control their own destinies)
- High levels of self-confidence

Previously, resiliency studies have focused on understanding resiliency in children. My original study considered how the construct of resiliency influenced adult targets of workplace bullying and if that affected how they coped with that experience. My findings suggested that the same factors that determine whether or not a child copes positively with traumatic life events can be useful in understanding how resilient adults will be as they adapt to and cope with high-risk situations.

As I listened to the stories of the targets' accounts of their bullying experiences, I thought how difficult, or impossible, it would be to rebound from such abysmal mistreatment. Their personal and professional standing in their organizations were threatened. They suffered emotionally, professionally, financially, and physically. Incredibly, many were resilient human beings who rose above the poor treatment.

However, resiliency is not just about being tough, strong, or smart. The targets I interviewed for both studies were tough, strong, and smart. In my first study, they were all university professors with doctorate degrees. Many are re-

https://doi.org/10.1515/9783111332260-005

nowned in their fields and have published journal articles, presented at conferences, and written books. Targets in my follow-up study had various backgrounds and worked in a myriad of industries. They were accomplished individuals. The major difference in how they coped with the experiences of being bullied was reflected in the factors that define resiliency.

On the other hand, being part of an organizational culture that legitimized bullying by failing to deal with it is a risk factor that may stifle resiliency. However, the people who shared their stories for this book demonstrated resiliency in the ways they coped with the bullying experience, both during the time it happened and later. They also discussed the emotional support they received from spouses, parents, and siblings during that difficult time. Finally, external support systems contributed to their resiliency. They formed an informal support group; they had close friends with whom they could share their experiences; and they had deep spiritual beliefs that helped them to know everything would be fine.

Steinhardt & Dolbier (2008) tested the theory that a person who is more resilient is better able to cope with life's stresses than a person who is not as resilient. They conducted a 4-week pilot study with college students. In this study, they investigated an intervention that was designed to enhance resilience, coping strategies, and other protective factors. First, they administered a survey to measure those factors. Second, in four sessions, they taught skills for problem-based coping strategies, taking responsibility, empowerment, and connecting with others. Then, they administered a post-intervention survey to measure changes in behaviors and perceptions. Their study concluded that resilience may be developed through awareness and training.

Most of this chapter about resilience is told by the targets in their own words. The goal is not to make people who are less resilient feel bad about themselves or to wonder what they could have done differently. The goal is to offer words of encouragement and to provide ideas from other targets about how they have thrived in spite of the bullying they experienced. Finally, I offer specific steps that psychologists offer to help people build resilience.

Evan's Resilience Story

Evan even said, "I think people handle things differently. I have a certain resiliency about me that enables me to look at the situation clearly and know that it is not about me. It is about the bully. However, there are people who may not be as confident or as resilient, and they may not handle things as well. They had some very personal consequences as a result of the bullying. I made a decision that I was not going to get too involved in the minutia and details. He tried to hurt me;

he tried to hurt the people who worked for me. In the grand scheme of things, life is just good and there is no way that he can harm me in a way that is going to stick. But he could do that to other people, and he did.

Spiritually, I have always had a strong belief in divine intervention. The way I see it, we are surrounded by angels who really are not dictating the circumstances of life. We do have free choice. But the angels are out there working, and when I hit a fork in the road, they pile enough garbage there, so they know I am going to choose the clean path. Sometimes I look back at life and wonder how I made this decision or that decision. But it was the exact right decision. It is not because I am brilliant at all. It was a decision based simply on some intuitive gut reaction, and it turned out to be exactly the right one.

When that happens often enough, I just have faith that there are things operating that I cannot see touch or feel, but I have faith that it is going to be fine. One way or another it will be fine. For me, it could also be that I have lived sixty plus years. If I was forty, I do not know how I would have reacted to all of this. It may have been remarkably different. I am sure I would have been more alarmed and running around like my hair was on fire. I am blessed to be at my new university. I am living the fantasy."

Hailey's Resilience Story

When asked how she coped during the bullying period, Hailey said, "I probably whined about it to my family. I talked to my kids and my husband, and they were really incensed. I knew I had their support. However, I mostly just got busy trying to drive more customers my way for my little part-time businesses. And I was trying to find another job opportunity.

I had people counting on me. I had to step up to the plate. I focused on seeing what I could do to find more work and bring in more income. I was the breadwinner. My husband was not working. We had just relocated to another state, and he was not able to find a job in his field. I just figured it fell to me, and I just better be focusing my energies on looking for more work. Instead of worrying about what was happening, I needed to concentrate on what needed to be. Resilience is key in my family. I have had an interesting and challenging life.

My philosophy is that resilience is a huge part of how we just keep moving forward. I shifted my focus from continuing to think about the negative experience to moving in a more positive direction. Resilience is essential to everything. Interestingly, the first class I took in my master's program focused on adults and the aging population. What I learned is that at the very core of a longer, happier, and healthier life, both physically and mentally, is resilience. I come from a family of strong women who have always been resilient. Many are single moms, so they had to be. I was a single mom with seven children and no child support or family help. I had to be resilient to survive.

Of course, when I was going through all of the trauma, I went through the steps. I thought is there anything I can do about this? I did not think so, and I remember at times feeling helpless. I also knew I did not have a choice. People were expecting me to take care of them. All I could do was move forward. For me, it was a matter of grit and determination. Maybe it is pure stubbornness. It is just a mindset.

I've got two favorite sayings and I think this has a lot to do with resilience, so I hope it is alright if I share those with you. My first favorite saying is 'the past should be a guidepost not a hitching post.' Since the first time I heard that saying I have attempted to live my life by it. Essentially, everybody has a past, but none of us have a future. We only have today. We have to move forward, and I only look back to see how far I have come. I use that saying to help me with my resolve to move forward. That is my first favorite saying.

My second favorite saying is from Lao Tzu; it is 'bend and overcome.' What that means to me is an image where I see a river peacefully running between the banks. There are bushes on the side. There is grass. There are some tall, strong trees. Out of the blue one day, all of a sudden, the river has a raging torrent that just washes everything out. It uproots the trees. It forces them downstream. It knocks the bushes out. The grass is buried in mud and debris.

And eventually the river goes back into its banks again after this flashflood. Trees are gone. The bushes are washed away mostly. And grass is buried. But as the mud and debris starts to dry out and crack, little blades of grass push up through the earth, and they bounce back stronger than ever because they were able to bend under the weight of that horrible flood and come back to rise again. I like to use that as a visual to remind myself that I am like a blade of grass. I need to be able to bounce back up when the flashflood is over. Between those two sayings, it really helps to strengthen my resolve to move ahead."

Sam's Resilience Story

Sam said, "I learned resilience from my father. He had similar bullying situations in his work life. Although at that time, no one called it bullying. He was able to let them go, and I always wondered how he did that. But I just thought, 'Well, if that is what you have to do, it is what you have to do.' He always had a positive attitude and he always bounced back.

On the flip side, I have worked at that organization for thirty years. I wanted to do other things, so I left there and did another business venture. That did not work out for me. Eight months later, I went into real estate, and I did that for about ten years. I am resilient, and I feel like if you persevere, you can overcome almost anything."

Jill's Resilience Story from My Other Study

Jill managed a professional office, and she talked about how she had landed her dream job. Before taking the position, a few people who were familiar with the office warned her of one particular person who had been there for years. Jill said, "I am a very positive person. I can get along with anybody. I could not understand why she disliked me so much. Through it all, I knew I was doing my job and doing it well. I took the high road, kept my integrity intact, and have stayed true to myself. I am known for supporting and building the practice.

I took charge of my own well-being. I had a lot of support from other people who worked in the office, not the leaders, but other people. I surrounded myself with supportive people. I chose to be strong and to stay positive. Don't get me wrong. It hurts, but I can either let the hurt consume me, or I can regroup, get my truth back, and get my strength back. I chose the latter.

When I agreed to interview with you, I hoped that by sharing my story I could make a difference. I wanted to be instrumental in bringing it to the forefront. It dredges up a lot of the feelings and the effects of that time, but if I can make a difference, it is all worth it."

Becca's Resilience Story

When sharing her story of thriving through the bullying period in her life, Becca said, "my confidence was shaken, and it was difficult to rebuild. Luckily, I have really good friends who stuck by me and helped me. I ended up finding another consulting job with another company. And, if you go into consulting, you have to build your business. At the organization where I was bullied, I had friends and other peers, and they helped me with networking and finding new businesses to connect with. With their help, I was able to move forward.

I also read a lot of self-help books. They helped me to shift my thinking and create a positive attitude. Just one of the authors I listen to a lot is Simon Sinek. For me, he has a great way of breaking things down to a very common level on friendly terms with analogies that make a lot of sense. I listened to his interviews and podcasts on YouTube, and he has two books, *Leaders Eat Last* and *Create Your Why*. These books helped me focus on my purpose. He worked with the military, and he talks about how in the military they are a team. From basic training, they are taught to cover for one another. No person is left behind. Everyone is in it together; everyone helps each other out of any situation. He links that mentality to corporate America. What if we all had each other's backs rather than trying to stab each other in the back? Organizations would be so much more productive.

One of the self-help books I read talked about whatever you put out into the world will come back to you. The experience of being a target of a bully helped me to work on myself and to put good positive energy out into the world. Working on myself and my attitude has helped me realize that I control my own destiny. I can let it beat me down, or I can become my best self."

Charlie's Resilience Story

Charlie, who was working for a brilliant and talented chef, said, that "the bullying taught me to be resilient and it taught me to prepare. And now, nobody yelling at me is ever going to make me feel bad because I have already experienced it at an extreme level. So, you learn to be resilient; you learn to prepare; you learn to handle criticism extremely well. Because when he is yelling and screaming at you, you cannot let it get to you because you still have a job to do. You just suck it up and move forward.

He did keep me focused; he did keep me moving. I survived. I even thrived. For example, when I was cooking on the line, I was performing at a level that I never thought was possible. And it taught me resilience. It taught me how to think outside of the box. I was put in situations that were outside of the comfort zone, and I found ways to survive and thrive in them. I guess he helped build my mental toughness.

I think he could read how far he could push people because there were some people who he just totally laid into. And then, there were people he kind of left alone. I don't know if bullies are sometimes able to see who they can get away with what. I think because I did have a resilience, he was able to throw more at me. Because others, he did not throw as much.

I was performing at a high level, and he ended up promoting me while I was working with him. I was in an a la carte restaurant and he promoted me to a supervisory position in the banquet department. When I was moved, they replaced me with two people, so that told me that I was performing at a pretty substantial level.

I think there are certain personalities that adapt to that situation differently and better, perhaps, than others. You know, life experiences give you the self-awareness to understand and to not let people have influence on you that way. Not that I am good or bad at it, but I think that there are some who are better able to do that than others.

I live my life the best I can, and I identify my own worth. I was lucky. I left that experience and got into another similar one with some of the same aspects. It is part of the industry. I rose above everyone else. I was resilient and I knew how to handle the situation when other people did not.

Then, I went to chef school, and I excelled. Any self-doubt he tried to put into my head was dissolved. I was reaffirmed by people who I also respected, and it helped me know my self-worth.

I am also a big believer that things happen for a reason. In my life, I have looked back at things. Totally random happenings in my life take on significance later on. I am sure that there were things that I experienced with him that were instrumental in my success later in life. And it is scary the way some of this stuff happens.

And so, I do not look back and wish I could change anything. I do not want to pull out the stinky garbage; that garbage is something I built my career on. And if those things had not happened, who would I be? How would I be different today? Where would I be going? What would I be doing? We all have a past and have things that have happened to us. But it is not the things that have happened to us; it is how we deal with them now.

Are you still bringing them up? Are we still pulling them out? Are we still letting them define us? Or are we saying, 'Wow, that happened, I survived it. I not only survived, I thrived.' Because I do think things happen for a reason. I look back and see these boulders on my path. I had no idea how I was going to get around them, but I always did. Sometimes it was a different path that was so much better than the original way I thought I was going.

Coming here is an example of that. I was at a very low point in my life, and I took this job that I never should have taken because it was not what I needed financially. I was moving to a place I had never considered. There were so many reasons for me not to take this job. But I did, out of necessity, because I was newly married, and I had a young child. And do you know what? Coming here is one of the best things that ever happened to me. And the only reason I am here is because I had a sous chef that I worked with in the past who was a graduate. I believe that the whole reason I met her was so that I would end up here. So, things happen for a reason."

Parker's Resilience Story

"Yeah, I mean, I would say I've had good things happen because of the experience not bad. I created a life based on what I went through to help others and that was my whole dissertation on understanding the motives of a perpetrator. Maybe that'll help something. I mean, it's a small thing. I teach domestic violence and anger management to perpetrators and I win every one of them over and their lives are better for having been through my classes. Ninety percent of the time. There's always one here and there that I make mad, because I make them follow the rules. But I had a guy graduate last night from class. He gave me a hug. So no, my life's better. Kind of grateful that all of that happened in a way."

Jack's Resilience Story

"There was an informal group of those of us who were targets. We got together periodically to just talk and support one another. Knowing we were not alone and that someone else understood what we were going through helped tremendously.

Also, the first thing I would do every day is look in the mirror and say positive affirmations, such as 'Today, I feel great. I am going to go in and immerse myself in my work with enthusiasm.' It might have been false bravado and that type of thing but that is what I would do. I kept a positive attitude. I would be the most enthusiastic and the most cheerful person in the room. The next thing I would do is remember my own self-worth. Every time I had a chance, I would go up to him, smile, and tell him all the things I was doing in my classes or in my research.

Every three years, the university replaced my computer. One year, I got one with a flat screen, and I wrote him an email just to say, 'thank you so much; I really appreciate it; it helps with my work.' I would just do stuff like that."

Building Resilience

Some researchers liken resilience to whitewater rafting down a river. Along the journey, we enjoy a slow, peaceful ride. Then, there are areas where the rapids are rough and challenging, much like life. Resilient rafters in the river of life take the journey with trusted friends who may have more experience navigating the waters, or they may wear their life jacket, so they are safe when the turbulence hits. As a result, they emerge from the ride more confident and courageous.

The behaviors of a workplace bully affect people differently. Some, as in my studies, adapt, gain strength, and move forward. As mentioned by several of the targets, the bullying was a painful and challenging time in their lives, but they realized they could not change what happened, nor could they change the leaders' reactions to it, so they refused to allow it to zap their joy and their zest for life. Others remain traumatized by the horrendous treatment, even years after it occurred. Resilience plays a factor in how well they adapt.

The good news is that resilience is not a personality trait that you are either born with or not. Rather, resilience can be developed by changing one's perspectives, thoughts, and behaviors. With time and thoughtful practice, it can be developed and improved. There are four core components that help empower people to withstand the rough rapids of life and circumvent life's stressors.

They are:
- Building connections
- Promoting wellness
- Finding purpose
- Embracing healthy thoughts

Building Connections and Promoting Wellness

Developing relationships with empathetic people who are trustworthy, compassionate, and who validate our feelings helps us know we are not alone. This might take the form of lunch with friends, connecting with a spiritual community, or participating in a civic or professional organization. In part, that may also be joining a team in a sports league, such as tennis or walking. This type of activity also helps to promote wellness, as exercise strengthens our bodies and helps us fight stress. Eating well and getting enough sleep are also ways to promote wellness. Celebrate any small accomplishments or goals met.

Finding Purpose

Seligman (2011) contends that trauma may destroy our self-confidence, our trust in others, and our hope for the future. One way we can overcome these negative reactions is to shift our thoughts. Look for opportunities to grow and develop because these can help you find purpose. According to his research, personal transformation comes from appreciating being alive, acting on new possibilities that life offers, improving our relationships with others, and deepening our spiritual connections. As difficult as it is, shift your thinking to those things in life you are grateful for, rather than the things that cause you pain (Newman, 2016). Visualize how you want your life to look, rather than focusing on the trauma.

This does not mean denying your emotions. Denying your emotions, staying angry, blaming others, isolating yourself from other people, and constantly reliving the pain, hinders, rather than builds resilience. Feel the anger and the hurt, but do not pitch a tent and live in them. Newman (2016) says that reliving the events over and over and rehashing the pain is like a cognitive spinning wheel that does not help us heal or move forward. Take back your power and work through the emotions. This is not an easy or flippant suggestion. It is admittedly a slow process that takes time and possibly professional help.

View the trauma as a fork in the road. Which path will you take? Consider how the trauma you experienced can help others. For example, if you know others who have been targets of workplace bullying, share your story with them. This lets them know they are not alone, and it helps you make connections with them (apa.org). Focus your attention on your strengths. Write them down and read them when you feel the negative reactions to the trauma creeping in.

Practicing Mindfulness to Build Resilience

Much of the research on developing resilience discusses mindfulness practices (Oh, Sarwar, Pervez, 2022; Newman, 2016; Seligman, 2011). Mindfulness is sometimes perceived as a nebulous or new-age concept, and its benefits are often discounted. However, practicing mindfulness provides stability and control over traumatic situations, and it encourages more positive emotional responses. As a result, we are less likely to respond negatively to situations.

Mindfulness helps us understand and be more compassionate toward others; it opens our hearts to being more self-compassionate. Through mindfulness, we realize that we are all interconnected. By living in the moment, we can recognize and let go of habitual ways of thinking and acting (Riskin & Wahl, 2015). When we are anxious or stressed, it is easy to slip into mind*less*ness, act on autopilot, and revert to our comfort zones of fight or flight, so acknowledge that mindfulness is a practice. As with anything, the more we practice, the more proficient we become.

Riskin and Wahl (2015) offer STOP as a simple tool that can be used to create mindfulness quickly and help us focus on what is important at the moment. STOP is:

S = Stop what you are doing
T = Take a breath
O = Observe body sensations, emotions, and thoughts
P = Proceed with whatever you were doing

Developing mindfulness takes practice. However, when we can live in the moment, we can begin to appreciate others' contributions, we practice compassion, and we lead by example. As a result, we more effectively address our emotions and overcome any obstacles that are preventing us from building our resilient muscles. To practice mindfulness, stop for a minute, focus on the present, and reflect on what is important in this moment. Be aware of your thoughts and your emotions. And just breathe (Wilkin, 2022).

Developing an Attitude of Gratitude: My Own Lessons

As I read the literature on building resilience, I was not surprised to see that shifting our focus to looking for opportunities to be grateful is part of that practice. Yet, I also thought that it could be challenging to tell someone suffering from the trauma of being a target of a bully to be grateful, even though some of the targets I talked to mentioned gratitude. I thought it might be helpful to share my path to cultivating an attitude of gratitude.

As humans, we have a desire to live a life filled with joy, peace, love, and abundance. Based on my own experience, one of the best tools for experiencing this life is to practice gratitude. I started this practice at a time in my life when it was challenging to find things to be grateful for. My trauma was not bullying, but the world might consider it something that was unforgivable. In retrospect, this seems to be the most unlikely time for me to develop a gratitude practice, yet that is exactly what I did. While this practice has been life-changing for me, please know that I am not here to tell you how to live your life. My goal is to simply share with you some of my life lessons and experiences. Feel free to implement what works for you and leave the rest behind.

Benefits of Developing an Attitude of Gratitude

As I examined my life and my attitudes about it, I recognized that I often focused on what was not going well. However, I learned that joy and peace are often a result of processing the world from the perspective of what I have and what is right. When I started my gratitude practice, my perspective and my view of the world changed. This required a real shift in my focus because sometimes, things on the outside do not feel like opportunities. There were times when I had to search for something to feel grateful about. However, when I opened my heart and mind, and when I aligned my thoughts with feeling grateful, I was able to experience more joy and less stress.

Here are my life's lessons I want to share with you.

Lesson # 1: What to Do When Life Looks Hopeless

Sometimes, it can feel like we are being buried by life's circumstances along with our emotional responses to those situations. I am reminded of a story about a man's favorite donkey that fell into a deep hole. He can't pull it out, no matter how hard he tries. So, he decides to bury it alive. Soil is poured onto the donkey from above. The donkey feels the load, shakes it off, and steps on it. More soil is poured. The donkey shakes it off and steps up. The more dirt was poured into the hole, the higher the donkey rose. By noon, the donkey was grazing in green pastures. When life happens, and it will, I have learned that I can either allow myself to be buried by the load of dirt being shoveled on me, or I can step up, learn something from the experience, and refuse to allow circumstances to define my happiness.

Lesson #2: Perspective – Change Your Thoughts, Change Your Life

My gratitude practice started with a shift in how I viewed the world. The more mindful I am and the more I practice gratitude, I begin to realize that when I live in and practice gratitude, I become more loving toward others because my focus is on my blessings, not lack. Change your thoughts, change your life. Did you know that 95% of the thoughts we have today are the same ones we had yesterday and the day before and the day before that? I often found myself on autopilot, mindlessly going through my day. Over and over, I reacted to the same situations in the same way. Shockingly, I was surprised with repeated life experiences based on my responses. I know that my mind is a powerful tool, and my thoughts and perspectives create my reality. On a daily basis, I started to ask myself:
–   What does my life look like?
–   Are my thoughts negative and limiting?
–   Are my thoughts positive and uplifting?
–   Do my thoughts inspire me to embrace and move through the day with ease, grace, and joy?

My answers to these questions helped me focus on building the life I wanted, and if I found myself slipping negatively, I could more easily focus on the good things in life.

This story demonstrates how our perspectives shape how we experience the world around us. It is about two gentlemen who were paraplegics. They had the same diagnosis and the same prognosis. One was lying in bed in a fetal position, railing against life and his fate. The other was out of bed, sitting in a wheelchair, explaining that he was grateful for a second chance in life. As he was wheeled through the garden, he realized that he was closer to the flowers and that he could actually see right into the eyes of his children. It is all about perspective.

Ralph Waldo Emerson once said that in order to achieve contentment, one should cultivate the habit of being grateful for every good thing that comes to you, and to give thanks continuously. Changing the way I view my world changes the way I feel and the way I act or react. Having an active gratitude practice created a fertile ground for peace and joy to grow in my life. And I found that when my attitude of gratitude became a daily practice, I started to draw to myself even more experiences that helped me feel peaceful and joyful.

Lesson #3: My Gratitude Practice

For me, gratitude is part of my daily life. Before I get out of bed every morning, I consciously bring to mind the people, places, things, and practices for which I am grateful. This may be my husband, my family, my friends, my spiritual community. I am also grateful for meaningful work where I get to make a difference in my students' lives. I also developed a practice of walking outside and experiencing the beauty of nature. When I walk, I am grateful for the birds, saying hello to neighbors, and the quiet solitude of my surroundings. Some people write in a gratitude journal.

Be aware that this is practice, and in the beginning, it may be difficult. When I am dealing with a difficult experience, I try to be grateful for the lessons I will learn from what is happening. I also use affirmations and denials when I am going through a difficult experience. My affirmation is, "The universe is conspiring to make all my dreams come true." If the negative feelings prevail, I deny that the experience or thought has any power over how I live my life.

Develop your own attitude of gratitude practice. Whatever your gratitude practice, you will cultivate and protect your joy and peace by training yourself to look for the good, to find the positive in everything, and to be grateful for all the good in life, even when it is tempting to do otherwise. Part of the beauty of gratitude is that it is like a magnet. The more I am grateful for, the more I have to be grateful for.

Chapter 5
Reacting to the Shattered Pieces of Life After the Bullying

> *I wanted to make sure it never happened to anybody else at that organization again. I cared less about money than my attorney did. I wanted an HR person installed, and I wanted some-body that had to make sure that no other person's rights were violated. So, I wouldn't settle until they could guarantee me that (Parker).*

The overarching goal of my original study was to explore and understand how people cope with the experience of being a target of a workplace bully. The substantive theory that emerged from that study was that targets are able to move from victim to survivor when they are enlightened or become enlightened and can change their reactions to the bullying behavior, release blame and anger, and empower themselves. They came to the realization that they cannot change the bullying behavior, nor can they change the leaders' responses to the behavior. In fact, changing anything external to themselves is impossible. The changes must come from within them.

This is the Theory of Enlightened Transformation. Enlightened means knowing that we do not have to remain stuck in victimhood. It is knowing that we have the power within us to transform our experiences by letting go of those things that do not help us live our best, most authentic lives. It is not allowing anyone or any event to control how we act or react. That knowing helps us to change the way we view the world.

Some participants talked about letting go of blame and anger. Others discussed their continued suffering and feelings of powerlessness, suffering, and traumatism. The survivors were self-confident; they advocated for others; they took responsibility for their own reactions; and they were not malleable. Conversely, individuals who continue to be victimized said they lacked inner strength; they looked to others to resolve the problem; they could not forgive the university leaders or the bully; and they tried to acquiesce and do what the bully wanted.

Each target of the bullying behavior in my first study was subjected to the same types of mistreatment. However, some targets have been able to move, while others still feel traumatized and powerless. A comparison of the faculty members who discussed being able to move on and those who say they are still suffering from the trauma revealed five key differences in the way they responded to the events. Again, every participant experienced similar behaviors, and all were initially angry that the leaders did not intervene to stop the bullying.

https://doi.org/10.1515/9783111332260-006

Moreover, each faculty member confronted the behavior and avoided the situation by either leaving the university or staying away from the bully.

Table 2 summarizes the Theory of Enlightened Transformation.

Table 2: Enlightened Transformation: Moving from victim to survivor.

Survivors	Victims
– Possess self-confidence	– Continue to search for reasons why they were targets
– Change their reaction to the situation or others	– Attempt to change the bullying behavior and leaders' reactions
– Become an advocate for others	– Look to others for help
– Develop empathy toward the bully and the leaders	– Continue to blame and be angry at the bully and the leaders
– Let go of blame and anger	– Seek revenge for the bully and the leaders

The concepts of Enlightened Transformation, self-confidence, reactions, advocacy, empathy, and letting go are not linear ideas. Rather, they overlap and build upon each other. Someone can be stronger in one area than another and still experience the benefits. Although I discuss the first four in this chapter, I devote an entire chapter to letting go of blame and anger.

Self-Confidence

Self-confidence is not arrogance. However, it is a belief in one's skills and abilities. As a result, confident individuals have an internal locus of control, and they do not allow life to happen to them. They are realistic about their strengths and weaknesses, and they capitalize on their strengths and work to overcome their weaknesses. Being confident does not make someone immune to adversity or to experiencing anger, frustration, and doubt when difficulties occur.

One attribute that the survivors shared was self-confidence. Although the bullying in their lives shook them to their core and briefly caused them to question why this was happening to them, they were able to realize that they were accomplished professionals who had a lot to offer. They were true to their authentic selves, and they consciously and intentionally created peace and harmony in their lives, refusing to let the bully threaten their inner peace. Conversely, the targets who were not coping as well with the experience mentioned how the bullying behavior caused old childhood tapes to play in their heads, which can blur the vision of their true selves. Parents, spouses, or others who were not always kind to them resulted in feelings of not being worthy. They had deep-rooted feelings from those early experiences. Some wondered what they did to cause the bullying. The truth is they did nothing to warrant being targets of the bully.

No doubt, it can be challenging to overcome the conditioning of our past and to move forward. However, the good news is that we can build our self-confidence and create that sense of peace and well-being. One way to do this is to silence the inner critic. Not only does our inner critic keep us from our peace, but it also can prevent us from experiencing opportunities in our lives. Imagine that every time you allow your inner critic to steal your peace, you pick up a heavy rock. By the end of the day, how many rocks are you carrying around? Our hands are so full of the heavy rocks of self-doubt and self-criticism that we are unable to enjoy the beauty of life.

Putting down the rocks or refusing to pick them up in the first place can be easier said than done. It requires a conscious and mindful shift in thinking. We know that we create our life experiences through our way of thinking. That inner dialogue has a lot to do with how we experience the world. Recognize the inner critic. Then, make a conscious effort to shift those thoughts to positive ones. Be kind and loving to yourself. Think about your strengths. What makes you unique? What talents are you offering the world? In times of self-doubt, refocus by answering those questions.

The Connection Between Vulnerability, Authenticity, and Self-Confidence

Employees at all levels of the organization thrive when they feel safe and respected and when they can be their authentic selves at work. Pixar, the animation studio that created movies such as Toy Story, Luca, and Elemental, fosters a culture where employees can be strategically vulnerable when their self-confidence is shaken. They created a mentorship program where mentors and mentees can honestly share experiences about their triumphs and challenges. Through this process, trust builds, positive collaborative relationships are built, and the mentors are more likely to advocate for the mentees as they seek advancement in the organization. As a result, mentees feel more confident, even during their vulnerable times.

The leadership recommends creating a psychologically safe culture where people are rewarded for being vulnerable, yet brave enough, to ask questions and admit they do not understand or know how to do a task. In part, this means becoming aware of biases and creating a more inclusive workforce that empowers everyone to feel safe in their vulnerability (Woolf, 2024).

Reactions

Another aspect of Enlightened Transformation is that the targets who were better able to cope with the experience discussed changing their reactions to being targets. Instead of trying to get help from the leadership, they started to shift their thinking. They realized that they could not change the past, and they had no control over what happened to them. However, they did have the power to change their individual reactions to the abusive treatment. The people who were better able to cope transformed their lives by moving forward instead of putting so much attention on the bully's negative behaviors.

Targets who continued trying to get help from the administration or to stop the Dean's behavior were stuck in victim consciousness (Hasselbeck, 2010). When we suffer in victim consciousness, we believe that we have no control over our lives. Things happen TO ME. At this level of consciousness, we feel powerless; we may be angry and resentful. Our moods are dictated by whatever is happening in the outer circumstances. We may be looking for revenge and thinking about how we can hurt the person. When we are in a victim consciousness, we don't get the peace we are seeking. We are stuck in the quicksand of hopelessness and helplessness, and we often cannot see a way out.

Victim consciousness happens when we hold on to the past, even though it no longer serves us. Sometimes, we choose to hold on to hurt feelings, painful memories, and resentment. We tell our old stories over and over again, and they become like a big old, smelly bag of trash that we drag along with us everywhere we go. Our mental energy and thoughts determine what we experience, and when we continue to feel like we are a victim of our circumstances, we will in fact experience being a victim of our circumstances.

When the targets looked for someone else to intervene, and no one did, they were overwhelmed with thoughts of hopelessness and disillusionment. Then, they became more frustrated, and every thought of frustration was like ordering a big old helping of more frustration.

Every thought that agrees that we are stuck is asking the universe to send us more of the glue that got us stuck. Further, when we put all of our energy into negative thinking, there is no space for positive, life-affirming thoughts and beliefs. The past is past, and dwelling on it, especially any negative experiences, is a waste of time and energy. Whatever happened cannot be changed. Although we cannot change the past, we can choose to let go of any error or limiting belief system; that system tells me I need to react in a particular way or that I should be hurt or offended. When we are in victim consciousness, we empower someone else to dull our sparkle. It is difficult to soar and to shine when we are weighed down with old beliefs.

Conversely, the targets who were able to change their reactions experienced victor consciousness. Victor consciousness happens when we understand that we are empowered with the freedom to change our reactions to our outer circumstances. Our thought is that our reactions are controlled BY ME. Without a doubt, all the targets of bullies were wounded deeply by the mistreatment. Victor consciousness does not mean that whatever happened did not happen. However, we do not have to pitch a tent and live in our misery.

Advocacy

One of the factors that contributed to helping the targets cope with the experience of being bullied was advocacy. Evan mentioned that one way he dealt with the bullying was to stand up for others and to ask how he could help them. Those actions helped him feel like he was doing something and making a difference. Likewise, Henry took measures to counteract the bullying by becoming an advocate and trying to help others. He said, "I did what I do with everything. I went around to everyone that I knew and asked what is going on. 'How can I help you?' I was not the only person. I was the main target at the moment, but he had all kinds of victims that he was trying to destroy. I wanted to let them know they had an ally, and I was here to help them if I could." In fact, participants in my first study all experienced being bullied by the same person, the Dean. In addition to Evan and Henry, Abby, Cara, Jack, and Grady all mentioned trying to reach out and help others who experienced the bullying.

Parker was a participant in my second study. In that study, each person was singled out by a bully, but others were not targeted by that person. As a result, her advocacy story is a bit different. She filed a lawsuit against the employer who bullied her. She said, "The bully crossed a line with me. At first, she was overly critical of my work, and she ridiculed me in front of my colleagues. Then, she forced me to come in during my time off. Whatever I did was never enough for her. Then, she started telling lies about me to people who were my friends there. I tried to remain positive, and I think that made her more abusive to me. Then, she did something that was illegal. Since I settled a lawsuit, I cannot discuss the details of that.

However, since I decided that not only was she really mean to me, but what she did was unlawful, I decided at some point along the way that I wanted to make sure it never happened to anybody else at that organization again. So, I cared less about money than my attorney did. I wanted a human resources position created and someone hired to fill it. Much to my attorney's chagrin, I would not settle until they could guarantee me that. In the end, it was less about me and more about making it better for everybody who currently worked or would work for that organization."

This advocacy is akin to vessel consciousness. Vessel consciousness happens when I acknowledge that what happened is not excused or condoned. However, I can become a vessel and use my experiences to help others. I can become an advocate for others who share the same experiences.

Empathy

One of the most surprising factors that contributed to how well the targets were able to cope with the experience of being a target of a workplace bully was empathy. Instead of continuing to blame and express anger toward the bully, several targets wondered what happened to that person that led to the mistreatment of others. The targets certainly did not condone or accept the emotional abuse. However, they tried to understand the motivations behind the actions. Empathy is a fundamental aspect of human interaction that not only improves our relationships with others but it also contributes to personal growth.

Worthington (2001) suggests that empathy requires connecting with the bully by attempting to identify with their feelings, emotions, and motives. Admittedly, this is not an easy task. In part, experiencing interconnectedness between you and the bully is a key to empathizing because it is the conduit that uncovers commonalities, strengths, and interests. The targets who were better able to cope with the bullying attempted to separate the person from their offense and to realize that all the facts about the bully's childhood or pressures at the time of the offense are not known.

Jill talked about trying to understand what motivated the bully. She said, "I knew she had issues. She was going through a divorce; she drank a lot; and she was on medication. She was an incredibly unhappy person. That's the way I look at it now. I am sad for her. She will never know what it's like to put love out there or to care about another person. You have to care about another person. What you give, you get so much more in return. To have somebody like that who is so isolated and who has so few friends living in the world is sad. I get just as much from being there for someone else. I cannot imagine what that would be like to not care at all."

While discussing the bullying in his life, Sam mentioned having empathy for the person who bullied him. He said, "in this industry, there is so much pressure, and there are a lot of bullies in healthcare. I tried to understand her position and why she did what she did."

Similarly, Charlie was in a profession where many bosses are bullies. When asked how he felt about the person who bullied him all of these years later, he said, "I almost pity him. He has continued with the abusive behavior, and it hindered his career growth. He was on a pronounced upward trend in the industry, and then he plateaued and did not progress any further. He developed a reputation for mistreating people, and there was a lot of turnover. That behavior is becoming less acceptable." Parker said, "As time went on, I got less mad at her, and I felt sorry for her. She got demoted, and she could never supervise anyone again. As far as I know, she retired."

Hailey said, "I did my best to feel sorry for her. I tried to phrase it so that I would feel bad for her that she would have to be so insecure that she would have to trash someone in order for her to feel better. I did that in order to try to refrain from my feelings of anger toward her. Mostly it just got to the point where screw it, it doesn't matter anymore. At some point it just didn't matter."

Their stories of empathy and how it facilitated their coping strategies, increased their self-awareness, emotional intelligence, and resilience. By regularly practicing empathy, we can develop a more profound sense of compassion toward others and navigate life's challenges with grace and understanding.

Conversely, Kameron talked about how she had no empathy toward her bully. She said, "I understand that he may have had a troubled childhood, but there comes a point in life where people take responsibility for their actions. You cannot go through life blaming your childhood. I think he had that choice, and he went to the dark side. I have no pity or compassion for him. I would be very happy if his life is miserable."

Letting Go

Targets of workplace bullying may find it difficult to heal while they hold on to anger, blame, and resentment toward the bully and the organizational culture that supports the bully. The overarching difference between the targets who were liberated from their initial pain and those who still feel anguished and tortured is the degree to which they let go of blame and anger. Targets who have moved past their experiences of being bullied have taken steps in the direction of emotional freedom. They no longer hold a grudge, seek vengeance, or harbor anger against the bully.

Charlie said, "I forgive him, but I have not forgotten. I just do not let it impact me. I'm not a psychologist so I cannot tell you what long-lasting damage it has done to my psyche. But I can say that in all honesty, I do not think of him often except for when I am trying to come up with bad managers examples. I reference him in my teaching because he is a great indication of what should not be done. Life experiences give you the self-awareness to understand and to not let people have influence on you that way."

Jill talked about forgiving both the bully and the organizational leaders. She said, "You have to move forward and forgive on so many levels. I look at her as the troubled person that she is. But I also had to find forgiveness for the bosses who had to make that decision and chose what they did because I felt like I was hurt twice, once by her and once by them. I also had to forgive myself. I was angry at myself for being in that situation, and not handling it in a different way. I tried for so long to handle it myself. Why did I let it go that long?"

Conversely, targets who still suffer are held hostage by pain and anger of the unjust treatment toward them. Kameron said, "I have some forgiveness work to do in this. It's hard for me to do. I have tried to put it behind me. But I don't know how to forgive him for ruining my career and for what he did to the children. I am not there yet. If he was sitting right here in front of me, I would tell him I am glad his career has been destroyed."

Brooke also said she could not forgive her bully. From her perspective, forgiving the bully would be the same as saying there was nothing wrong with what she did.

Claire discussed the anger she still feels toward her bully, and the bullying events that happened 8 years ago. She said, "I have not forgiven. He made my life so miserable, for so long, and every time that forgiveness comes up in scripture, in church, or in meditations, I think about it, and I'm just not ready to do it. I can't do it." When asked what forgiveness means to her, she said, " It means letting go of what has happened to me, wishing good things for the person who bullied. I am not forgetting it, because I think that you can forgive without forgetting. Those two functions are totally different. One is aligned with your heart, and one is intellectual. And so, I think just forgiveness would be realizing it happened, and it is over, so I can move on. I cannot do that. I have so much anger. It is not hatred. I do not hate anybody. But I have so much anger and resentment."

It is interesting to note that Claire had been bullied as a child by her mother, and she also felt bullied by her ex-husband. She talked about how mistreatment from so many people hurt her self-confidence and self-esteem. She did not have the confidence or the power to stand up to the workplace bully. She lost her job, and she was still grieving the loss of the job, of the income, and of the camaraderie she felt with her co-workers. By the end of our interview, she was talking about how it helped her to see that forgiveness was a possibility, and she truly hopes she can do that before she leaves this earth.

Applying Enlightened Transformation

The Theory of Enlightened Transformation is not about making the people who are not coping well with being bullied feel bad. Rather, it was generated based on the stories and experiences of targets. The goal is to provide hope to targets and to give them suggestions on how they might shift their thinking to bring more peace and harmony to their daily lives. In reality, most of us experience all the levels of consciousness on a daily basis; if we tend to live more in victim consciousness, we have the freedom to either keep doing what we are doing or to make another choice and react in a different way.

The enlightened in Enlightened Transformation begins with awareness and being mindful of our feelings and emotions. It is the knowing that we do not have to remain stuck in victimhood or in any area of our lives that does not bring us peace and joy. It requires us to turn off the autopilot we sometimes use to get through our day and to be aware of the present moment. To live in the now.

Sometimes, it is simply convenient and comfortable to live life going through the motions. Although it is convenient, it could also mean our lives are out of balance. To create balance, we have to extend our thoughts into the world that matches what we want to see in our own lives. Thoughts of being disconnected or thoughts of revenge create vengeance and disconnection. Our thoughts have to match the energy we desire. If we want to be loved, treated kindly, and be respected, then we approach everything and everyone from a place of love, kindness, and respect.

Transformation is being willing to change if what I am doing does not result in living my birthright of joy. Transformation is an opportunity to embark on a journey of self-discovery and inner transformation. Consider your unconscious patterns and beliefs. Which ones serve you and which ones would you like to replace?

Advice from Targets

In both studies, I asked the targets to provide advice for others who are targets of workplace bully based on their own experiences. Henry said, "Those of us who were the most vocal came out basically unhurt. Faculty members who were more vulnerable suffered more. The Dean was a clinical psychologist who knew how to get to people's weak areas. And he took his punches. He did not encourage them to continue their growth and to be the best person they could be. I think my advice would be to not be so afraid. Fear is not in your best interest. Most importantly, band together and support and advocate for others." Becca offered, "gather your strength and have the self-confidence to stand up for yourself." And Claire's advice was "do not just curl up and accept it as your lot in life. That is not healthy."

Several people mentioned getting professional help. Lily said, "once it becomes apparent that the leaders or administrators are not going to do anything within the system to save you, find a way to save yourself. Self-care in the form of a professional will provide a safe place to talk it through, share your feelings, and begin to rebuild your self-confidence." Grady also advised speaking with a therapist who can help you work through the trauma, and Cara concurred. Sometimes, the feelings of powerlessness and disillusionment are too much to handle alone. Professional help may alleviate some of the long-term effects. Becca also counseled that if after talking to the leaders and others, if the stress is still too much, seek professional help.

Similarly, talking to others who are experiencing bullying will help you know you are not alone. Grady said, "small groups of people getting together and talking to one another and listening to people's common stories is helpful and therapeutic." Becca mentioned finding alliances with others and sharing your stories. Do not keep it bottled up. Claire added talking about it with friends and family would be helpful, and definitely talk about it with like-minded people.

Abby advocated the importance of speaking to the bully as soon as you recognize that the behavior is bullying. She said, "tell the person you hope we can stop it right now and you want to work in a culture that is free of this kind of behavior. Make it really clear to the person that you will not stand for it. To do that takes a lot of courage and you have to rehearse it ahead of time. Every time I went in to talk to the Dean, I rehearsed it beforehand. He had an uncanny ability to just absolutely take over everything that you were saying. He would turn things around and take you in a completely different direction. I would say to the person be very clear and direct about what you want to say and what you want to change. And then, continue to follow up if the behavior continues.

If your one-on-one conversation does not stop the behavior, bring the faculty in or other employees in a gentle way and just say, 'I feel like I am in an environment that feels hostile to me. Maybe the rest of you are not experiencing this, but I would like to know if you are, and I am just wondering how we can change the atmosphere.' Put it on the table in front of the bullies and in front of the other victims. I did go directly to the Dean, and I think because I confronted him, I suffered less. I saw more vulnerable people suffer a whole lot more. He did hideous things to them. And do not assume the administrators or leaders will take care of the problem. Do not assume it will just go away. We really did believe it could not get any worse, and it just continued to get worse. If you talk to somebody and nothing happens follow up and follow up again."

Jill advised addressing the behavior with the leadership early. She said, "I tried to fix it between the bully and me. Then, I was afraid to go to the leaders because I knew it would just get worse and be more convert. Get facts together so that you can present your problem. Those people are incredibly manipulative. I suffered in silence for too long. Then, when I finally brought it to the leaders' attention, they were incredulous about how I could let it go on for so long. At least I would have felt like I was in control. I would have been able to say, 'this is what is happening to me.'

I would have had an answer about whether or not they were going to support the bullying. If they were, I could have taken charge of my own well-being and moved on for my own physical and emotional health. Just do not let it go on for too long without addressing it. It is not worth the toll it takes versus having that courageous conversation."

Sam and Claire both advised against displaying anger when you confront the bully or bring it to the attention of the leaders. Claire said, getting angry about it and digging your heels in is not going to get you anywhere. Sam concurred, saying his number one piece of advice was "do not act in a state of anger. Just step back, evaluate, and try to understand why that other person did what they did."

Charlie said the most important thing he did for himself was to let it go. However, he said, "in all honesty, you cannot tell people to just let it go. They have to make that decision when it is best for them. I am not living their life, so who am I to tell them do that. They will do it when they are ready. My best advice is, 'When you're ready to give it up, give it up. And then just let it go.' Holding on to all of that anger is only going to hurt you. The bully does not care, so you are not hurting them. But honestly, until you reach that point yourself, it is never going to happen. I think it's presumptuous of me to tell you to get over it. You will when you are ready."

Cara recommended documenting everything. She said, "whether you want to stay in your position or you want to leave, it is good to have everything that happened in writing. You can leave with your good record and a couple of good recommendations. Or if you are going to stay, and this was actually my mistake, just say put it in writing every time they do something to you. When two of the Dean's chosen tormentors, Lou or Hazel, asked me about a situation, I should have asked them to send me an email, and I would respond to it. It would have given me evidence of my conversations."

Chapter 6
The Wounds Are Deep: Healing Through the Practice of Forgiveness

Forgiveness is about letting go. I made the conscious effort to free myself from the chains of hostility and negativity because that is really a downer to live with. Who wants to live like that? Not me! (Hailey)

The Theory of Enlightened Transformation attempts to explain why some targets of workplace bullying let go of the trauma and survive the ordeal (or even thrive), while others suffer, continue to relive the bullying events, and are still victims of their experience. In the words of the participants, the overarching difference between the targets who were liberated from their initial pain and those who still feel anguished and tortured is the degree to which they experienced the concepts in the Theory of Enlightened Transformation; this Theory includes the following elements, as I detailed in the previous chapter:

1. Demonstrating self-confidence
2. Changing reactions
3. Advocating for others
4. Developing empathy
5. Letting go of blame and anger

All of these elements are encompassed by forgiveness. Forgiveness is the adhesive that connects all the elements.

Targets who have moved past their experiences of being bullied have taken steps in the direction of emotional freedom. They no longer hold a grudge, seek vengeance, or harbor anger against the bully. Conversely, faculty members who still suffer are held hostage by the pain and anger of the unjust treatment toward them.

There is no judgment in holding on to that anger. Targets of workplace bullies are deeply wounded by the behaviors of the bully. This was certainly the case with some of the targets of the bully in my study. Some targets lost jobs they loved. One lost her career. They experienced shame and humiliation at the hands of the bully. Friends sometimes avoided them. A few faced health challenges. Some divorced. The actions of the bully changed the course of the targets' lives.

Interestingly, no one in my original study used the word forgiveness. Yet, as I discussed the results with my dissertation Chair, she advised me to look at Molly Layton's Model of Forgiveness. Layton's three-stage model provided a clear delineation between the individuals who were better able to cope and the ones who

https://doi.org/10.1515/9783111332260-007

were still traumatized. Most likely, anyone who is abused or mistreated goes through all of these stages. Hopefully, this model may serve as a beacon to help targets move from victim to survivor. Here are the stages:

1. Stunned innocence
2. Tortures of obsession
3. Transcendence

In the stunned innocence stage, targets often search for the meaning and purpose of their pain, shame, and suffering. At this point, targets question why they were sought out and attacked. *Forgiving the bully helped them get past this stage; each of the targets who forgave the bully stated it was a process.* They started at this stage where they could not believe what was happening to them, and they questioned if they perceived the behavior incorrectly. Unfortunately, when targets are unable to move past the stunned innocence stage, they continue to relive the experience, carry anger and blame, and suffer from the unjust behavior they have experienced.

The next stage is obsession which is characterized by trying to hold the person or the people behind the behavior accountable for their actions. In part, they look to others to help them right the unjust treatment they have experienced. The targets who moved on from this stage started advocating for others, while those who still suffered looked to the leaders to resolve the bullying problem. The leaders' failure to do this exacerbated the feelings of helplessness and hopelessness for those who have not been able to let go of the anger and blame.

When individuals reach Layton's transcendence, the final stage, they look inward for the change that will enable them to move past their experiences. They recognize the change must come from within themselves. They cannot change others' behaviors; they can only change their reactions to the behavior. The targets in both studies who were able to move on recognized this, and they let go of their desire for revenge and their anger toward the bully and the organizational leaders.

The research supports the positive physical and psychological benefits of forgiveness (Butler & Mullis, 2001; Madsen, Gygi, Hammon & Plowman, 2009; Fehr & Gelfand, 2012). Jampolsky (2011) says that forgiveness is the answer to almost everything. Given the positive benefits of forgiving, why is forgiving so difficult to do? In part, there may be a misconception about what forgiveness is and what it is not. Additionally, some people may want to begin their forgiveness work, and they simply do not know how to begin.

What Is Forgiveness?

Richard Enright, at the University of Wisconsin Madison's International Forgiveness Institute, credits Joanna North (Enright & North, 1998) with conceptualizing the ideal of forgiveness, and these components inspire their work. These components are that people who have been hurt:
– Have a right to feel their pain and be angry;
– Acknowledge the other person's behavior was unfair;
– Know they deserve respect;
– Offer the person who hurt them the gift of compassion, benevolence, and love, even though they may not deserve it;

Forgiveness is replacing or giving up the ill feelings we have for another person, situation, or even ourselves and replacing those with peace and harmony. True forgiveness is gifting (the giving part of forgiveness) ourselves and the offender by letting go of anger, bitterness, and resentment toward the person who has caused us pain. Therein lies the paradox. The target's freedom comes from gifting the offender with forgiveness (Enright, 2001). Forgiveness is letting go of the past and starting down the path to inner peace and freedom.

Forgiving the Unforgivable

Make no mistake about it. Forgiveness is often not an easy choice, especially when the actions of the other person seem unforgivable.

When I first started studying forgiveness, I read about a gentleman named Everett Worthington. Dr. Worthington was the Executive Director of the Campaign for Forgiveness Research at Virginia Commonwealth University, and he devoted his life to studying and promoting the benefits of forgiveness. In 1995, his mother was brutally murdered by an intruder, and his philosophy of forgiveness was put to the test. While pacing the room one night, he debated with himself the pros and cons of forgiving. He was understandably angry, and he did not want to extend the gift of forgiveness to the person who senselessly and viciously changed the face of his family forever. However, his research and his life's work had taught him that carrying around the burden of blame, anger, and resentment creates and exacerbates pain and heartache. It is like hauling around a red-hot coal with the intention of one day throwing it back at the one who hurt you. He recognized that only someone who was extremely damaged could commit such a heinous act. He chose forgiveness.

Benefits of Forgiveness

Forgiveness is a powerful tool that can replace anger, fear, blame, and discontent with hope, joy, peace, and contentment. When people choose to forgive, they enjoy enhanced peace of mind, improved relationships, and better physical health. Forgiveness scholar, Robert Enright, says forgiveness is as important to the treatment of emotional disorders as the discovery of penicillin was to the treatment of infectious diseases. Living life and being controlled by the past does nothing to change what happened. It simply takes the joy out of today. When we allow the person who hurt us to be a constant presence in our lives, we give our power to that person. When we hold resentment toward someone, we are bound to them by an emotional link that is stronger than steel. Another forgiveness scholar, Richard Holloway, contends that the real beauty and power of forgiveness is that true forgiveness gives us back our future.

Conversely, choosing not to forgive is akin to deciding to go through life carrying a hot coal of bitterness, resentment, blame, and anger, just waiting to throw it at those who offend us. While we are holding onto it, our own hands and our hearts get burned and scarred. Nelson Mandela, who spent 27 years in prison for opposing apartheid, said that as he walked out of the prison door toward freedom, he knew if he did not choose to leave the anger, hatred, and bitterness behind, he would still be in prison. When we continue to live in the past and tell our story of hurt and grievances, it is as if we are dragging around a big, smelly bag of trash with us everywhere we go. Then, every now and then, just so people do not forget, we take out a piece, show it to others, and say, "isn't this awful"? If we drive down the highway of life always looking in the rearview mirror, we will crash.

Myths About Forgiveness

So, if forgiveness is the answer to moving past being a victim, if it gives us back our future, if we can replace anger and blame with joy and contentment, why is choosing forgiveness so difficult? Why do we hold on to blame, anger, and resentment? What is preventing us from opening that space in our hearts to healing, peace, love, and joy? In part, there are myths about forgiveness that prevent us from embracing and practicing the concept.

– Myth #1 – Forgiveness means condoning or justifying what happened.
Forgiveness is not sending a message that the action was OK, and in fact, it was not OK.

– Myth #2 – Forgiveness means forgetting.
Forgetting is impossible, and the relationship between remembering and forgiving is part of the forgiveness process. To tell someone who has been abused or harmed to forgive and forget sends a message that their story is not important, and if we cannot tell our story about what happened, we cannot begin the healing process. Memory denied or ignored is like an untreated infection. It festers and threatens our physical and emotional health. Furthermore, the past does not just magically go away. Remembering may not be easy, but forgetting is impossible.

– Myth #3 – Forgiving is as easy as saying, "I forgive you."
Forgiveness is work. It is a process.

– Myth #4 – We need an apology before we can forgive.
Apologies are not prerequisites for forgiveness. In some cases, the person simply is not sorry or does not see how they caused any harm. Other times, the person may no longer be on this earth, so an apology is impossible. If forgiveness were dependent upon an apology, we would be stuck with anger and resentment and all the negative repercussions that come with them. Fortunately, that is not the case.

– Myth #5 – Forgiveness means reconciliation.
Again, not true. Although forgiveness has the power to transform relationships, forgiveness and reconciliation are two very different concepts. Forgiveness can occur without reconciliation. However, reconciliation without forgiveness is insincere. While resentment and anger dissipate with forgiveness, it takes trust to reconcile, and it requires a positive view of the future relationship. Forgiveness is aimed at the person, not the act, and anyone involved in an abusive relationship or has been deeply wounded should make every effort to leave that relationship.

– Myth #6 – Choosing forgiveness is a sign of weakness.
Contrary to this belief, Holmgren (1993) theorizes that only a person with high levels of self-confidence and self-esteem can work through the process of forgiveness. Further, her work reinforces other bodies of research that contend releasing the chokehold of anger and resentment (the basis for genuine forgiveness) makes room for joy, excitement, love, and gratitude. These positive emotions help empower the people who forgive and reward them with increased self-respect (Holmgren).

– Myth # 7 – The other person does not deserve to be forgiven.
We believe we were hurt so deeply that the bully does not deserve forgiveness. The prevailing thought may be that they deserve to be hurt the same way we were hurt. The truth about forgiveness is that it is a gift we give to ourselves, not to the bully.

Foundational Research on Forgiveness

Foundational forgiveness researchers, Everett Worthington and Robert Enright, offer two separate models to help people work through the process of forgiveness. Forgiveness is not an act of will that can be accomplished through sheer determination. Although the desire to forgive is the vehicle that drives the act of forgiving, a transformational process that replaces the negative emotions with positive ones is imperative. Worthington (2001) proposes the Pyramid Model to REACH Forgiveness. The acronym REACH stands for:
– **Recall** the hurt
– **Empathize**
– Offer the **Altruistic** gift of forgiveness
– **Commit** publicly to forgive
– **Hold** on to forgiveness

According to Worthington (2001), injustice, violations, and pain manifest themselves in either a fight or flight reaction, and neither is productive. Therefore, the first step in the healing process requires acknowledging (**Recall**) the hurt and anger. The initial important first step has been taken toward forgiveness and healing when feelings of anger and blame begin to dissolve.

The next step on the forgiveness journey is **Empathy**. Admittedly, this is not an easy task. In part, uncovering the interconnectedness of the two parties is key to empathizing because it helps uncover commonalities, strengths, and interests. Additionally, Worthington suggests that empathy requires connecting with the offender by attempting to identify with that person's feelings, emotions, and motives.

The next step in Worthington's model is offering the **Altruistic gift of forgiveness**. He says that the benefits of forgiveness are only realized when it is given freely and unconditionally.

Worthington suggests that publicly **Committing to forgive** brings accountability to the process. Telling a counselor, relative, friend, or even the offender about the decision to forgive gives it credence and solidifies it in the forgiver's mind.

Finally, anger and blame are natural reactions to being hurt, so **Holding on to forgiveness** will likely require repeating one or more of the steps in the model. However, forgiveness provides intense emotional relief from holding onto the negative emotions.

The final step in both Worthington's (2001) and Enright's (2001) models of forgiveness is holding on to forgiveness, which manifests itself in a changed attitude. At this stage, the forgiving individual begins to realize that he or she is gaining emotional relief from the process of forgiving the offender. He/she may discover that the meaning behind the suffering is an increased capacity for compassion or a new purpose in life.

Likewise, Robert Enright (2001), in his Process Model of Forgiving, contends that there are four distinct phases of the process, which are not rigid, and some individuals will experience all or only some of the stages. These stages include:

- Uncovering
- Decision
- Work
- Outcome/Deepening

At some point, the forgiver realizes that holding on to the past is not productive (**Uncovering**). They make the decision to move forward (**Decision**), and this is the impetus that drives the process to the next stage. This is where the real work begins (**Work**). It requires a paradigm shift and the pursuit of a more peaceful life that is not bogged down by the events of the past. Enright suggests that looking at the world though the other person's lens will help separate the person from the offense. The forgiver acknowledges that facts about the offender's childhood or pressures at the time of the offense are unknown. The paradox of forgiveness is that the forgiver is empowered and healed (**Outcome/Deepening**).

Create Peace

Listening to the experiences of the people who were able to forgive and, as a result, cope more effectively with being a target of a workplace bully, I developed the acronym CREATE PEACE (Wilkin, 2023) to expand awareness of the benefits of letting go of blame and anger, to work on the process of forgiveness, and to create more peace in our lives. It encompasses Worthington's (2001) and Enright's (2001) models and extends those concepts to acknowledge the experiences and stories of the targets.

C – Choose to Forgive

The first step on the path to forgiveness is making a conscious choice to let go of any past grievances. This desire to forgive is the very heart of forgiveness work. As with any journey, the first step is often the most difficult. Letting go of anger and resentment paves the way for positive emotions, such as joy, excitement, love, and gratitude. This choice requires a willingness to not only let go of past grievances but also eradicate the desire to hurt others. By choosing to forgive, we no longer find value in our stories about how others have treated us. Although blame is the path most traveled, moving in a different direction toward releasing anger and embracing forgiveness will lead to peace of mind and contentment.

R – Remember the Emotions

It is important to remember and acknowledge the pain and emotional distress caused by the injustice and the violation because healing cannot begin until we process the emotions. We are emotional beings, and we will feel angry or resentful when we are hurt, when trust is broken, when others try and dull our sparkle. We cannot simply say, "go away anger and resentment" and poof it dissipates. Expressing anger can be good.

If we deny it, we are also denying our pain. Give yourself permission to feel and to be angry. Do not deny it or stuff it down. Repressed, unexpressed, or harbored anger will steal our peace, our joy, our health, and our enthusiasm for life. In fact, if the emotions are ignored or denied, they will manifest themselves in a continuous state of victimization. What we resist persists. Anger and resentment are like venom that courses through our bodies after we have been bitten by a snake. It is not the bite that kills you; it is the venom. You can remove and drain the venom by expressing anger and resentment and then choosing to let go of any emotions that do not serve you.

While feeling and acknowledging emotions is vital, it is critical that we do not pitch a tent there and live in negativity. Harboring anger and resentment means we likely will continue to relive the experience and continue to be a victim of what happened to us.

E – Empower Yourself

If we only focus on our wounded feelings, we give the person who hurt us power over our lives. Forgiveness allows us to take back our personal power. When we feel stuck in a situation and we tell our stories looking to others for help, if they do not sympathize or react the way we want them to, we may experience feelings of helplessness and hopelessness. We allow them to live rent free in our heads, and we are building an invisible wall that breaks our connections to one another. It can be difficult to experience our connections with other people.

It can be easy to look outside for others to fix the problem. There is a popular story of a woman on a street late at night, searching on her hands and knees under a bright streetlight. A man walked by and asked her what she lost and how he could help her. She replied, "I lost my key, and I am looking for it." The man gets down on his hands and knees and begins to help the woman look for her key. After some time of unsuccessful searching, he asks the woman where she lost her key, and she replies, "I lost it inside." Then why are you searching for it on the road? She replied, it is dark inside, but there is a brilliant light on the street, so I am looking for it here. Although we may laugh at that story, sometimes that is basically what we do. We often look for someone else to do something to help us find our peace and joy. The reality is that the only place we can find it is within ourselves.

A – Altruistic Gift of Forgiveness

Forgiveness comes with no strings attached. It does not rely on an apology or promises from the other person that the behavior will not be repeated. Forgiveness transforms us into loving beings. The paradox is that we offer compassion and love to the person who hurt us, knowing full well that the offender does not necessarily have a right to those gifts. In reality, forgiveness has nothing to do with the other person. We are the ones gifted by forgiveness because we are freed from anger, blame, and resentment. We are gifted with our futures.

T – Transform Your Life

Transform your life by giving up your victim story. Put down the big bag of smelly trash you have been dragging along behind you. Change the story you tell. Invite love, joy, peace, and contentment into your life. Even when we may be justified and have a right to be angry, holding on to that can block our healing and keep us locked in victim thinking. When we release living in the past and start living in the present, we begin to write a new chapter.

E – Expect Life to Change

When we begin to write that new chapter, we can expect life to change. We cannot fill our cups with peace, joy, love, and harmony if it is overflowing with anger, bitterness, guilt, and resentment. Forgiveness offers happiness and a sense of peace. Forgiveness allows us to see the beauty in the world around us. To quote a Course in Miracles, "forgiveness offers a quietness that cannot be disturbed, a gentleness that cannot be hurt, a deep abiding comfort, and a rest so perfect, it can never be upset." Who would not want this?

P – Persist

Forgiveness is not a one-time event. It is a process, and it takes time. We go through the steps and the stages over and over and over again. There is no time limit; there is just progress. Forgiveness may require changing your belief system. Depending on the offense, you may have lost self-confidence. Your beliefs are your reality, so observe any negative self-talk and release that. Keep reminding yourself that you are an amazing person with unlimited potential and a true purpose in life. Consider that your mind is like a garden, and if you do not deliberately cultivate flowers, weeds will grow without much effort. So, plant and cultivate positive thoughts. Daily affirmations are a great tool for this.

E – Empathy

Forgiveness does not mean condoning or justifying what happened. It does not send a message that the action is acceptable. Consider what happened in the person's life that made them act or treat others that way. Yes, I know, easier said than done. How does the world look through the other person's lens? There is a wonderful quote by Martin Luther King, Jr that is a profound reminder about the power of love and forgiveness. He said, "He who is devoid of the power to forgive is devoid of the power to love. There is some good in the worst of us and even the best of us misses the mark sometimes. When we discover this, we are less prone to hate our enemies" (n.d.)

A – Advocate

Others in the same situation may need our emotional support. Advocate for them and offer to help them, especially if you are further along in the forgiveness process. Some of the participants in both studies found peace and purpose when they advocated for others who had experienced bullying.

C – Co-create

We cannot change the past. The third stage of the forgiveness process is transcendence. In this stage, we begin to look inward and recognize that this is the only place change occurs. We cannot change what happened, but we can change our reactions to it. The beauty and power of forgiveness is that it gives us back our futures. We have the power to transform our lives, and we consider the joy of co-creating your future with Spirit as your constant partner.

E – Enlightenment

Enlightenment is the knowing that we have free will to take control and to change our lives. It is comforting to know that we do not have to remain stuck in victimhood. We can know that we have the power to transform our experiences by letting go of those things that do now serve us and embracing a life overflowing with love, peace, and joy.

The golden thread running through forgiveness research and models is that anger, blame, and resentment are psychologically and physically detrimental to the people who have been hurt. Therefore, releasing them and replacing those emotions with more positive ones is fundamental to becoming enlightened and transforming the lives of the aggrieved. In part, this journey begins with a paradigm shift away from the myths about forgiveness, such as requiring an apology, condoning the behavior, or the need to reconcile. Forgiveness takes courage and confidence. The forgivers open a space in their lives to create a more joyful and peaceful life.

Chapter 7
Repairing the Damage: The Journey from Victim to Survivor

We are all inventors, each sailing out on a voyage of discovery, guided each by a private chart, of which there is no duplicate. The world is all gates, all opportunities. (Ralph Waldo Emerson)

Previous workplace bullying scholars (Adams, 2014; Namie and Namie, 2003) offer techniques to employ for targets who are experiencing the trauma of workplace bullying. These techniques approach workplace bullying from a position external to themselves dealing with the bullies and organizations. This approach is different from the Theory of Enlightened Transformation, but it has excellent ideas, nonetheless. I will reconcile the two approaches in this chapter. Initially, however, I want to discuss the steps used in the techniques of these scholars; there are four steps in this approach, which I will review below.

The first step is to keep records of exactly what happened, when it happened, and who (if anyone) witnessed it. One of my study participants, Jill, agrees with this advice. For years, she tried to deal with the bully by being kind to her or avoiding her. Others in the office witnessed what happened and often empathized with Jill. However, she loved her job and thought she could handle the bullying, so she did not bring it to the attention of her bosses. When things became unbearable, and she decided to have a conversation with the bosses, they were skeptical of her accounts. They wondered how she could put up with the abuse for so long without telling them. Detailed records would have helped her document the behavior.

The second step is to confront the bully. Namie and Namie (2003) suggest taking someone with you to the meeting. Practice what you will say. They recommend an assertive approach that lets the bully know you are taking back your power. There is power in numbers, so invite others to be part of that meeting, and use the detailed records you kept so the bully knows you are serious, confident, and strong. While being assertive, it is important to be ethical and professional and avoid threats of retaliation that could harm your reputation. However, according to Adams (1992) be aware that this approach may not work if the organizational leaders are not willing to take action to stop the bullying. It is interesting to note that between my two studies, twelve of the nineteen targets confronted the bully to no avail because the leaders valued the bullies' contributions or perceived contributions more than those of the targets.

https://doi.org/10.1515/9783111332260-008

The third step is to file internal complaints and go through the proper channels. This may mean filing a grievance, reporting the incidents to human resources, or going directly to the organizational leaders. Again, this may be futile if the leaders are either apathetic or if they do not know how to handle the situation. In fact, Namie and Namie (2003) warn that filing a complaint against the bully may result in targets being ridiculed, discounted, or accused of not being credible. In my first study, nine of the ten targets filed grievances, and not a single person had a positive outcome. Remember, Evan was told to either end the process and get what he wanted or continue it and receive nothing. Moreover, the leaders discounted all of the reports of workplace bullying and said they were unsubstantiated.

The fourth and final step is to know your rights. Several countries have laws and regulations against workplace bullying, and we will talk more about this in the next chapter. It may be necessary to explore external options, such as filing a lawsuit. Parker's bully crossed the line into harassment, and she filed a lawsuit.

Parker's story began when her boss became furious with her when she found out she was pregnant. When she went on maternity leave, her boss insisted that she come in and take care of something. She took her 2-week-old baby to the office with her because he was too young for daycare, and she worked for three days getting things caught up. She went back on maternity leave, but the boss kept calling her to come in for one thing or another. The boss would scream at Parker and bark orders at her in front of people. In the end, she was fired because her boss said Parker told her during an interview that she never intended to have children.

Parker won the lawsuit but was awarded only a small amount of money. However, the main thing she wanted (and received) was for the organization to establish a human resource department so no one else would have to have their rights violated and endure what she did. She refused to settle until they agreed to that. Parker said that the experience was horrific. In fact, it broke her heart to leave an organization whose mission was near and dear to her, but it also put her on her path to a new career in mediation and conflict management. She said, "Based on what I went through, I created a life where I help others through their trauma." She had a heartbreaking experience and turned it into a career of advocating for people who may not have a voice. She found her authentic self.

What Is Your Authentic Self?

I use the term "authentic" frequently in this chapter. It may be challenging to understand in all contexts, but I thought I would try to define it in terms of how I use it. Our authentic self is our "real" self without regard to how we appear to others. It means understanding our perspectives and perceptions about life; it also means accepting those perspectives and perceptions without judging or questioning our intentions. If you live according to your authentic self, you will not be sidetracked in your life's purpose by other people or events; you will be who you really are doing and what you are intended to do in this world.

Enlightened Transformation in Action

All of the above are strategies that people who are targets of a workplace bully can employ. However, they are external actions that people can do, and they often do not stop the bullying behavior. In addition, those strategies do not heal the hearts and souls of the targets. The goal of both of my studies was to explore how the targets themselves could restore their lives and rise above the trauma that they experienced.

As mentioned in previous chapters, the heart of the Theory of Enlightened Transformation is the thrivers and survivors realizing and sharing that they know they cannot change what happened to them. They cannot change what the bully did, nor can they change how their leaders responded to reports of the bullying. In their own words, they recognize that their power lies in changing their reactions to the experiences. This does not mean they simply accepted the mistreatment. However, they decided that even though they were initially devastated by the events, and they experienced feelings of hopelessness, helplessness, and powerlessness, being a target of a bully did not define who they are as a person.

In fact, they asked me to share their journeys from victim to thriver so that others who have similar experiences will have hope and know that they can move through that devasting time in their lives. They mindfully decided that if they allowed the person who hurt them to be a constant presence in their lives and if they lived from that space of blame, resentment, fear, and anger, they were giving the bully the power to continue to cause them harm. Catherine Ponder, in her book, *The Dynamic Power of Healing*, says that when we hold resentment toward someone, we are bound to them by an emotional link that is stronger than steel. The thrivers made the conscious decision to cut that emotional link and to free themselves from the pain of negative thoughts and beliefs that no longer served them. They mindfully worked toward creating a more authentic life. This chapter provides guidance for targets to help them with their journeys from victims to survivors and thrivers.

What Enlightened Transformation Is Not

One misconception of Enlightened Transformation is that as it shifts the power to the target, it may seem to excuse the bully's behavior. That is simply not the case. However, the thrivers truly understood that they had no power over changing other people's behaviors. Moreover, they could not travel back in time and change what happened. As a result, they empowered themselves to change their reactions to the devastating, gut-wrenching, and life-changing experiences. As you have read their stories in the previous chapters, this was a process, and it did not happen instantaneously. They were confident individuals who attempted to work within the system by reporting the behaviors to the university or organizational leaders; they filed grievances; they advocated for others. In the end, they believed they had two choices. They could carry their anger with them like that hot coal, or they could let it go and not allow it to continue to sear their souls.

The other misconception about Enlightened Transformation is that it is victim blaming. Nothing could be further from the truth. Targets of workplace bullies are victims of mean spirited, vindictive, harsh, and unfair treatment. No one deserves to be treated that way. However, once they become the target and experience mistreatment, it cannot be undone. The thrivers in both of my studies looked deep inside themselves and knew that if they changed their reactions, they could move forward, heal their lives, and create a more peaceful existence. This is what they chose to do.

Moving Toward Self-awareness and Conscious Living

The thrivers in both my studies shared certain attributes and took specific steps to overcome their trauma. They used phrases such as "living authentically," "letting go of toxic emotions," and "being kind to others." Sometimes, the journey was two steps forward and one step back. Through it all, they persevered, they became more self-confident, and they regained their power. The overarching theme of their thriving after being a target of a workplace bully is that their journey to Enlightened Transformation took them on a path to self-awareness and conscious living. Like forgiveness, this takes time and work. How did they accomplish this? Each had a slightly different approach, and the following are some of the practices they made part of their daily lives.

Conscious Living Begins with Self-Awareness

Living consciously is to intentionally be aware of what is happening in our lives and respond knowingly; this is self-awareness. When we find ourselves unconsciously just reacting to life's events, we can shift our focus from mindless, fear-driven feelings to a conscious state of mind. In part, we can practice self-reflection and self-awareness. Ask ourselves why do we feel the way we feel? What needs to happen for us to change our feelings and thus our thoughts? How can we practice being empathetic and kind to others? Robert Brumet, in his book, *Living Originally*, calls this radical self-awareness, which requires us to be aware of our experiences in each moment and to be conscious of our mental, emotional, and physical responses to those experiences. In essence, radical self-awareness goes beyond seeing and hearing to considering the significance we attach to each of those experiences.

Benefits of Self-Awareness

The word *enlightened* in Enlightened Transformation requires us to turn off the autopilot that we sometimes use to get through our day and to intentionally be aware of the present moment. When we become more self-aware, we will begin to appreciate everyone and everything in our lives. Everything in life shows up to teach us something.

An example of how one of my study participants became more self-aware is Parker. She discussed being emotionally and financially devastated by being the target of a workplace bully. Yet, she also said that she was grateful for the experience because it helped her have compassion and empathy for others who were in her situation. She was not happy to be a target, nor was she condoning the bully's behavior. However, she has made it part of her life's mission to help others through traumatic times in their lives.

Another example of gaining self-awareness is Evan. He feels blessed to be at his new university. It is a small school, and the architecture and physical plant are breathtaking. He said that there is a strong sense of community and collegiality there, and the students build lifelong friendships. He feels as though he is living his fantasy and doing what he was meant to do in this world with his perfect job.

An additional benefit of becoming more self-aware is that we begin to feel connected to one another. If something is destructive to one human, it is destructive to everyone. When we know we are all connected, we will be more compassionate and empathic. Jill experienced being self-aware and developed compassion for her bully. She never tried to retaliate or to strike back. She said, "It is not my responsibility how she treated me, but it is my responsibility how I treated her. There are people, I believe, who aren't capable of giving more. It's sad to me because she's in such an isolated life. She has no friends. She had a daughter who moved away. She kept trying to convince her daughter to stay because she would be lonely. I wonder what's inside her that would make her be that angry and mean spirited? I feel sorry for her."

When asked what she would say if she had an opportunity to speak with her bully, Hailey said, "If she was sitting in front of me, I'd probably say I don't know if you remember me, but I used to work with you. I just wanted to find out how you're doing. You know, are you okay? Are you still working at the hospital? Are you still in the same position? Have you been able to move on? How's your life going?."

As we become more self-aware, we start to experience balance in our lives because we are living more authentically, being who we really are, and we become more joyful. When we are self-aware, we know the truth of who we are right now. The past no longer has a grip on us, and we do not worry about the future. We know that joy is our natural state, and our conscious connection to the world around us helps us know that we are on our purposeful path. We will be less judgmental and more forgiving. We accept others as being on their own paths, even if it is different from ours. Just as our own perceptions and meanings are shaped by our experiences, it is also important to be aware that others' awareness and perceptions are shaped through the lens through which they view the world.

What Does Consciousness Look Like?

Louise Finlayson says that at its core, consciousness is pure compassion. On the flip side of that unconsciousness is fear. Conscious living manifests in our lives as:
- Being kind to ourselves and others;
- Being present in the moment;
- Being open to new ideas;
- Being willing to forgive;
- Being aware that we are all connected;
- Being grateful for every experience in our lives;
- Being compassionate and empathetic;
- Being unattached to things or outcomes.

She says when we unconsciously and mindlessly allow life to happen to us, we may suffer with the following experiences:
- Worrying about the past or the future;

- Carrying on an inner dialogue of self-criticism;
- Excusing selfish behavior;
- Judging or resenting others and holding a grudge;
- Trying to control situations or change other people;
- Gossiping or criticizing other people;
- Stereotyping people who are different from us;
- Speaking harshly to others or ourselves;
- Believing we do not have choice.

Going through life consciously with self-awareness manifests as the peace and harmony we long for in life. On the other hand, unconscious living manifests as reactions to what is going on in the world outside of our internal being; those reactions may be knee-jerk reactions to fear.

Eric Butterworth in his book, *"Celebrate Life,"* says that life itself is consciousness. You stand where you do today, wherever that is, because of your consciousness. And there is only one way you can come to stand anywhere else – by changing your consciousness. If you wish to go up higher, you can do so, and there is no limit to the heights to which you can climb.

Being conscious is also being aware of the present moment and moving on from the past. Targets of workplace bullies have a story in which it is easy to get caught in rehashing the past. The thrivers told their stories, but they did not allow their histories and the bullies' behaviors to define them. Worrying about the past leads to anxiety and stress. Wayne Dyer, in his book Secrets for Success and Inner Peace, uses the analogy of a speedboat to talk about our personal history. When a speedboat moves across the surface of the water, there is a white foamy froth behind it that is called the wake. The wake is nothing more than the trail that is left behind. The wake does not move the boat forward; that is the engine. He suggests applying this idea to our lives. The wake or the history of our lives is nothing more than the trail that is left behind. It is absolutely impossible for the wake to move our lives forward.

Conscious living, self-awareness, and living from the inside out, rather than the outside in, are keys to Enlightened Transformation. We often look for that elusive peace and harmony outside of ourselves, when the only place we can find it is deep within ourselves. It is comforting to know that we do not need the external world to access our peace. Finding peace within ourselves enables us to live authentically.

Living Authentically

Our authentic or real selves are joyful, loving, kind, and compassionate. If you doubt that, focus for just a minute on something that presents itself as less than peaceful in your life. Notice how you physically feel. Now shift your awareness to your idea of peace (a beach, the mountains, a sunset or sunrise, music, a field of wildflowers, a rushing waterfall). Notice then how you feel physically.

What happens in the outer world can rob us of our joy and prevent us from being our authentic selves, at least temporarily. The thrivers in my studies became enlightened and discovered their authentic lives. Their journeys started with a calm and peaceful life prior to the bullying, went through the turmoil and chaos of becoming a bullying target, and ultimately recovered and took steps to regain their power. Part of that journey was to rid themselves of damaging emotions that inhibited their advancement to Enlightened Transformation.

Releasing Emotions That No Longer Serve Us

Things happen, and they cannot unhappen. The targets in my studies experienced dark times, and they took a journey on an emotional roller-coaster ride as they suffered deep despair one day, and the next day held out hope for a better tomorrow. The thrivers began to experience more hopefulness than despair. They stopped giving the bully permission to live rent free in their heads.

Releasing toxic emotions is not easy. Often, those emotions are attitudes that are habituated over a lifetime of focusing on what is wrong and missing in our lives. In fact, did you know that 95% of the thoughts we have today are the same ones we had yesterday and the day before and the day before that? It is easy to run on autopilot as we go through our day, and we react to the same circumstances in the same way.

Our minds are powerful tools, and we use our thoughts to create our reality. What does your life look like? Are your thoughts negative, limiting (and untrue) self-talk? Or are they positive and uplifting thoughts that inspire you to embrace each day and move through it with ease, grace, and joy? Changing the way we view our world changes the way we feel and the way we act or react. If we can switch off the autopilot, we can break those old habits. One way to do this is to monitor our thoughts and feelings and ask ourselves whether our thoughts and self-talk are really true. The key and the challenge are finding ways to channel those emotions into positive outcomes.

Releasing toxic emotions does not mean we ignore, excuse, or condone how we are feeling. In reality, if we do any of those things (ignore, excuse, or condone), we get stuck on that never-ending roller-coaster ride. It can become easy to allow toxic emotions and events that were part of our past to rob us of our inner peace. Frequently, some of my participants would say, based on what happened to them, "I have a right to be angry, hurt, resentful." And that is true. However, when we carry resentment around with us and it becomes our constant companion, and those heavy rocks we are carrying weigh us down. We are allowing other people to manipulate us, and we are giving our power and our peace away to the very people who hurt us.

When we harbor toxic emotions, we may believe we are building a wall of protection around us. In reality, that wall prevents us from experiencing the peace and harmony we desire. Those emotions become our own personally constructed prisons. As counter intuitive as it sounds, tearing down the walls and releasing the negative emotions allows us to focus on our needs and shift our thoughts to what we do want and away from what we do not want. We accept ourselves for who we are, and we begin to accept other people for who they are, not who we think they should be.

When toxic emotions are preventing us from living authentically and stopping us from doing what is ours to do in this world, it is time to begin the journey toward letting them go. The first step to releasing fear, anger, blame, resentment, shame, or any of the emotions we may feel as a target is to acknowledge that we feel this way. Do not judge others or ourselves for these feelings. Simply feel.

Acceptance is the only place where change can begin. The Dalai Lama said, "Why be unhappy about something if it can be remedied? And why be unhappy about something if it cannot be remedied?" This does not mean denying what exists, nor does it mean resigning ourselves to circumstances. Acceptance allows us to move into joy as we surrender and accept life's trials on their own terms, rather than protest because our experiences are not what we expected. Stress, anxiety, and dissatisfaction come from our expectations of how we thought life should be. When we accept and surrender to the fact that we cannot change what happened, our journey is far less turbulent. We soon realize we have the power to change our future reactions to what happened.

Trauma, like that associated with being a target of a workplace bully, can overshadow everything in our lives. It is difficult to be conscious and mindful and to live authentically when we are waiting for the next emotional attack. Targets experience a spiral of emotions ranging from anger to frustration to shame. They may be consumed by the "what ifs." What if they say or do something that triggers the bully? What if they are embarrassed in front of their coworkers? What if they lose their job and their financial stability?

Not only can stress and worry lead to ill health, but it can also paralyze us with fear of the future or fear of change and keep us from living our authentic lives. The thrivers in both studies refused to let their very legitimate fears stop them from living their lives. They refused to allow anger to be their constant companion.

Make no mistake, fear and anger are real, and they are ugly. The thrivers did not simply deny their fear and anger. They acknowledged those emotions, and they did not pretend to be happy or positive when that is not how they felt. Fear and anger are natural responses to workplace bullying because someone is trying to hurt us, and we may feel powerless to do anything about it. Conversely, fear and anger can have a positive impact, as well. According to Harvard Health, fear and anger are not just emotions. In fact, we have physical reactions that trigger our flight or fight response to the threats. Physically, when we are angry or fearful, we may experience:

- Pounding heart rate;
- High blood pressure;
- Intense breathing.

Anger and fear can be helpful when they motivate us to leave a toxic workplace or relationship, advocate for others, resolve a conflict, or do something that will be both rewarding and satisfying. However, they can also deprive us of our inner power.

Taking Back Your Power

Workplace bullying can have a profound psychological effect on targets, and it can be difficult to take back your power after being subjected to the trauma associated with being a target. When shame, blame, anger, and fear are daily companions, the journey to becoming a thriver is difficult. In fact, trauma affects people in different ways. While some are better able to move past the damaging impact of psychological violence, others struggle with releasing toxic emotions, living consciously, and taking back their power. They are not too weak or overly sensitive. They are simply processing the trauma differently. For those targets who are struggling every day to let go of blame and anger, forgive, shift their thinking, and take back their power, there is hope. They can train their brains to release what is no longer serving them and to free themselves from the bullies' chokehold on their lives (Fraser, 2022).

Practicing Shadow Work to Take Back Your Power

One way to let go of ineffective feelings and positions is through shadow work, which is a concept developed by Carl Jung. It is the process of uncovering the unconscious aspects of our personality that we often reject or ignore because they are either too painful to confront or they bring up memories that we would like to leave in the past. Unfortunately, avoiding them does not make them go away. Self-awareness, the cornerstone of Enlightened Transformation and starting the journey toward thriving, is also an integral part of shadow work. Bullies trigger toxic emotions, creating feelings of inadequacy, and insecurity, and these reactions result in a downward spiral that exacerbates the target's suffering. When targets recognize these triggers and their emotional responses, they can become aware and be better able to manage their reactions and, in turn, neutralize the bully's power over them (Chappell, Cooper, & Trippe, 2019).

One of the most challenging aspects of shadow work is accepting that we have these hidden or unconscious aspects of our personality. In fact, resistance is a natural response to confronting painful parts of ourselves. If we can shift our attention from an obstacle to thoughts of what the lessons to learn are, we are one step closer to healing and empowerment. When we embark on this journey of self-discovery through shadow work, we transform unconscious reactions, experience personal growth, and reclaim our power. There are specific shadow work exercises that help us begin the process. They include:
– Journaling and other creative outlets;
– Meditation and quiet time;
– Affirmations and positive thoughts;
– Support and connections.

Journaling allows us to discover both strengths and vulnerabilities. It provides an opportunity to reflect on our life's journey and mindfully write down thoughts, emotions, and experiences. While journaling, consider past traumas or joyful experiences. What events or interactions trigger emotions, both positive and negative ones? Are there patterns of behavior? Are some emotions stronger than others? When we recognize and acknowledge why we experience certain feelings, we can decide if they are serving us or if we need to release them (Chappell, Cooper, & Trippe, 2019).

Meditation is a powerful tool for self-reflection. Evan meditated and focused on the positive ways he could help others. In addition, Evan was offered a job at a different university, and he said he never considered moving on until the bullying started. When he finally left for another position, he realized how oppressed he was and that the new job offered him opportunities beyond his wildest dreams.

To get started in your meditation practice, find a quiet, peaceful place and just be. Beginners may find it helpful to use guided meditation, listen to calming music, or practice in nature. Here is a five-step guide for mediating.

Step 1: Relax – Close your eyes. Relax, breathe deeply, and let go of outer concerns.

Step 2: Concentrate – Quiet your mind by focusing your thoughts your breathing.

Step 3: Reflect – With an open mind and a receptive heart, feel at peace.

Step 4: Embrace the Silence – In the silence, let go of any negative thoughts.

Step 5: Give Thanks – Be grateful for everything.

Sometimes, during meditation, it is difficult to focus, and our minds wonder. When thoughts arise, acknowledge them without judgment, and gently return your focus to your breath. There is no right or wrong way to meditate. It is a skill that develops with practice.

Affirmations and positive self-talk sound like solutions that are too easy to make a difference. Yet, they do. Jack used positive affirmations. He purposefully looked in the mirror every day and told himself he was worthy of all the good coming his way. Affirmations shift negative thoughts to positive ones. They reflect the goals we have for ourselves. Some examples are:

- I change the world one act of kindness at a time.
- I am living my authentic life.
- I am the peace and joy I want to see in this world.

Those are just a few examples. Words are powerful, so find an affirmation that works for you and say it out loud.

Self-talk, the internal dialogue we hold with ourselves, plays a significant role in shaping our perceptions, emotions, and behaviors. Whether we realize it or not, our self-talk influences our perceptions of the world. It also shapes our confidence in our own abilities. Positive self-talk is a powerful tool for personal growth and well-being. By cultivating a compassionate inner dialogue and being kind to ourselves, we can transform our mindset and navigate life's triumphs and challenges with resilience and enthusiasm. Pay attention to your words and thoughts and shift limiting ones to ones that inspire you. Sam said he remembered the advice from his deceased father, and that helped him through those dark and difficult days. His father taught him that his perspective and the way he looked at the world would determine his experiences. When he felt sorry for himself, he remembered that when his dad was alive, he would remind him that there is someone who is living through something worse. That guidance helped him to move on and not let the bullying define him.

Shadow work is a deeply personal process, and the self-discovery journey may bring up emotions that are difficult to work through on our own. Seeking professional support or counseling can enhance the process and help targets work through painful memories that the shadow work brings to light. Sophia recalled her experience with counseling. She said, "I had completely repressed this part. My mom died right in the middle of the bullying experience. She and I did not get along very well. She was kind of a mean girl, too. When I went back to school in the fall and one of the bullies started doing all of this stuff, and I was getting down, pretty upset, crying. I happened to have my annual physical with my doctor, and she recommended that I go to someone for therapy."

The therapist diagnosed Sophia with Post-Traumatic Stress Disorder Syndrome related to the way her mother treated her. The things that happened in her childhood that caused problems with her mother were being transferred to the bullies. She said, "I am not a crier, but when they were doing these things to me, I cried like a child. It was really amazing, and I not only dealt with all of the stuff that was going on, but also the history with my mother that bothered me for all of those years."

It is also helpful to connect with other targets and discuss how they coped with the experience. Grady, Abby, Sophia, and Alex often had dinner after work to share their experiences. For them, it helped to have someone to talk to who understood what was happening to them.

Shadow work is a deeply personal and sometimes challenging transformation process, so treat yourself kindly as you go through the process, proceed at a pace that is comfortable to you, be patient with yourself, and release any self-judgment. The benefits of shadow work are that it encourages self-compassion, emotional healing, and empowerment. It also leads to resilience, and targets will be less vulnerable to external stressors.

Practicing Kindness and Expressing Empathy

Practicing kindness and showing empathy were the final traits that thrivers shared. Evan and Henry, Abby, Cara, Jack, and Grady all tried to help others who were targets of the bully. Parker's resolve to not settle her lawsuit until the firm hired a human resources director illustrates how her focus was to prevent this from happening to other people. Her attorney told her she was "sitting on a gold mine," but she said money was not her motive. She wanted to protect others. Jill tried to help the bully when they were shorthanded at the office. When her bully had an accident, she sent her a beautiful edible fruit arrangement. Interestingly, the bully admonished her for this. Jill said, "She let me have it for that. She told me I should have sent a bottle of wine. She did not want the fruit and she told me I wasted my money because she just threw it away."

The other thrivers also had empathy for their bully. Parker said, "I felt sorry for her. She got demoted. She was no longer in charge of training and all of the social activities for the organization. She got demoted and she could never supervise anyone again. Her life was sad, and I feel like if she had been happier about life in general, she would not have treated people that way. As far as I know, she retired." Similarly, Becca said, "I'm sure she's been through something in her life that has caused her to be the way she is, and I feel sorry for her." Jill also mentioned that her bully was a troubled person who had a terrible life.

Evan said that after everything that he experienced, "The irony of the whole situation is after the fact I really didn't have any hard feelings toward the Dean. He is a flawed individual. He talks a lot about his history. His mother was insane, and his dad died. He grew up poor. Who knows how much of what he says is true, but what is apparent is he absolutely does not have the capacity to trust anyone. The whole time I was wooed and seduced and working with him and feeling like he is my friend I finally realized that the way he operates is no matter who you are, you are going to screw him. Someway, somehow, someday you are going to screw him. His mentality is that he can never fully trust anyone, and if the opportunity arises, he will get you before you get him."

Enlightened Transformation in Brief

The enlightened in Enlightened Transformation begins with awareness and being mindful of our feelings and emotions. It is the knowing that we do not have to remain stuck in victimhood or in any area of our lives that does not bring us peace and joy. Transformation is being willing to change what we think and do if our current habits are not creating the life we want. Transformation is an opportunity to embark on a journey of self-discovery and inner transformation.

Chapter 8
Preventing Workplace Bullying: Cutting Edge Practices to Bully-Proof Organizations

You can't go back and change the beginning, but you can start where you are and change the ending. (C. S. Lewis)

The overarching objective of my research agenda, beginning all of those years ago when I met Anna, has been to help the targets of workplace bullying. Initially, I explored how targets coped with the experience of being bullied and why some are further along on their healing journey than others. Honestly, I thought I would find that the thrivers practiced self-care, had a strong circle of family and friends, and possibly were supported by their spiritual beliefs. While I did discover that these things were true, the surprising findings were that they developed empathy for the bully; they advocated for others; and they chose to forgive the bully rather than harbor anger and blame. They were enlightened to realize that the trauma they experienced at the hands of their bullies and the administrators who did not stop it could not be undone. As a result, they changed their reactions to the behavior.

Those findings inspired my next study. Why would a target choose to forgive or choose not to forgive a workplace bully? The results of that research circled back to the findings in my original study and helped to confirm them. No matter how deep the wounds, they did not want to hold on to the hot coal of toxic emotions.

My goals for this book were threefold. First, I promised the participants in both my studies that I would tell their stories. Workplace bullying is emotional and psychological abuse that wounds the souls of the targets. The targets who participated in my research are brave souls with caring hearts. Some are recovering; others are still suffering. In the words of one of the participants in my first study, "the university is broken from within." They were saddened by what they endured at the hands of the bullies and the leaders who either failed to take any action or who decided it was easier to separate the target from their job than it was to deal with the bully. The targets had a deep need for validation and to have their voices heard.

Second, I wanted to help targets deal with the aftermath of bullying behaviors. Every target deserves an opportunity to thrive after being the target of a workplace bully. Targets who are currently being bullied may be able to use the experiences of the targets in my studies and apply the Theory of Enlightened

https://doi.org/10.1515/9783111332260-009

Transformation to their own lives. I hope that telling the targets' stories in their own words has helped accomplish these two goals.

I also want to help organizational leaders address the problem, and in this way, possibly prevent potential targets from suffering from future bullying. This is the third goal of this book and the focus of this final chapter. In fact, leaders can take control of the negative effects of workplace bullying by creating an organizational culture that does not condone or tolerate bullying. Organizations are responsible for recognizing and stopping workplace bullying, and leaders who fail to do that should be held accountable for the economic and human costs associated with bullying behavior. Since leaders powerfully influence the organizational culture, leaders' attitudes and actions will determine whether bullying behavior is accepted and tolerated or eradicated from the organizational culture.

Providing information about how to help organizational leaders is complicated because even scholars do not agree on how to accomplish this. It is not surprising that there is not a singular approach to addressing, managing, and eliminating workplace bullying. No doubt, this is a complex problem, and dealing with it requires multifaceted and intertwined strategies. Workplace bullying is not a one-size-fits-all problem, so there is not a one-size-fits-all solution. Duffy (2020) proposes a holistic strategic approach to addressing the problem of workplace bullying that includes, in part:

- Learn about workplace bullying;
- Acknowledge that workplace bullying can happen in your organization;
- Take reports of bullying behavior seriously;
- Ensure that dignity and respect are engrained in your organization's values, mission, and vision.

Some organizational leaders make a conscious choice to ignore bullying behavior because they view it as a tough management style. Some do not address it because they place a great deal of value on a particular skill or ability the bully brings to the organization. Conversely, other leaders either do not recognize workplace bullying behaviors or do not know how to intervene in a bullying incident.

There are internal processes, such as policies, skills, and awareness-based training, that help promote a workplace where people are treated with respect and dignity. Many times, targets suffer in silence, rather than report the bullying behaviors, especially if they fear nothing will be done about it, or if they report it the behaviors will intensify or become more covert. Targets need to feel they can safely talk about their experiences and that the leaders will listen and act on that information. Therefore, as noted in the *De Gruyter Handbook of Organizational*

Conflict Management, the first step on the journey toward reducing or eliminating workplace bullying is to shine a *LIGHT* on the problem (Wilkin, 2023).

How Leaders Can Shine a Light on Workplace Bullying

Learning about workplace bullying is crucial to addressing and preventing it. The targets in my studies reported that the leaders woefully underestimated their reports of the bullying, even dismissing them as individuals who simply did not get along with one another. Leaders can learn about workplace bullying, the consequences of sanctioning it, and the impact it has on targets by reading earlier chapters in this book. Moreover, the targets in my studies worked at a myriad of organizations, including universities, in professional offices, in healthcare, in non-profit organizations, and in consulting firms. Workplace bullying can happen in any organization. Accepting this possibility heightens leadership awareness and encourages consistent efforts to reduce it. Educating oneself and acknowledging the possibility that it can happen in your organization opens the door to taking reports seriously.

Managing the Conflict

As mentioned earlier, not all conflict is workplace bullying, but all workplace bullying is conflict. Furthermore, unresolved or mismanaged conflicts can escalate into workplace bullying. As a result, a strategic approach to conflict management is a step in the right direction for helping all employees recognize that they have a shared responsibility for creating a psychologically safe and respectful workplace (Duffy, 2020).

When productively managed, conflicts provide opportunities for us to shine our lights on the situations, develop more effective processes, and build collaborative relationships. To illuminate the conflict, we can incorporate the following concepts, represented by the acronym LIGHT (Wilkin, 2023), into our strategic conflict management practices:
- *L*isten to perspectives;
- *I*nvite Diverse Ideas;
- *G*enerate a psychologically safe workplace;
- *H*one a mindfulness consciousness;
- *T*hink about emotional reactions.

When leaders *LIGHT* the way, they model these strategies for others. They build positive working relationships that result in improved communication, respect, productivity, collaborative problem-solving, and empathy. This sets the tone for a compassionate organizational culture. Employees are more motivated and productive because they can focus on the organization's vision, mission, and goals, rather than being sidetracked and consumed by the possibility of being psychologically attacked by the bully. Additionally, they are strategies everyone can use when they are faced with a conflict situation (Wilkin, 2023).

Listen to Perspectives

Communication and perceptions are the underlying components of all conflict (Wilmot & Hocker, 2001), so listening to various perspectives is the basis of managing organizational conflicts. Meanings, perceptions, and responses to conflicts are created based on an individual's social realities and experiences. Often, people act competitively or cooperatively depending upon the lens through which they view the communication, the perspective of the situation, and the perception of the people involved (Kilmann, 2023). Instead of compassionately listening to others, we tend to filter our communication through our own lens of assumptions and biases (Kilmann, 2023). It is too easy to judge others as selfish, lazy, or close-minded when we do not understand why they act or interact in certain ways, or when we have not taken the time to understand their perspectives. We may think that our viewpoint is the only correct one.

We have been taught to believe that if we see it with our own eyes, it is reality. The truth is that the lens through which we view the world can skew what we see. The following image is a powerful depiction of why it is important to clarify the perspective of not only what we see but also what the other person sees.

What do you see? (Mi, 2013).

No matter how they tilt their heads or how long they look at the image, some people only see the young lady, while others only see the old one. The picture, of course, contains an illusion of both. Even when the participants only see one or the other, it does not change the reality that both are there.

Opening our hearts and being willing to listen and understand why others have different perspectives can shine a *LIGHT* on opportunities to learn, grow, expand our understanding, and resolve conflicts. We can gain a new and different perspective (Wilkin, 2023).

*I*nvite Diverse Ideas

One might think that since communication and perceptions are at the root of most conflicts, if we master listening to perspectives, we could eliminate conflicts. While that is a good beginning, it is also important to build on that concept and to invite people to present diverse ideas for problem-solving. People are more likely to buy-in to solutions when they help generate them. In fact, one of the pillars of facilitation as a conflict management method is creating ideas, and although that is a more formal problem-solving process, inviting diverse ideas and solutions is something we can all do when faced with a conflict. Schwarz (2002) contends that when we brainstorm ideas, it is important to not evaluate them, to include the wildest ideas, and to generate as many solutions as possible (Wilkin, 2023).

Listening to diverse ideas is especially important as organizations create anti-bullying policies. Start with collaborating with key stakeholders at all levels of the organization, and involve them through the entire process, from creation to implementation. Both organizational leaders and employees need to have confidence in the policies and know that the purpose is to protect all employees, and being part of the solution creates buy-in and improves their confidence in the policy (Wilkin, 2023).

*G*enerate a Psychologically Safe Workplace

A psychologically safe workplace is an environment where employees know they will not be humiliated or penalized for sharing ideas, asking questions, voicing concerns, or making mistakes. In a psychologically safe workplace, employees are more likely to be authentic because they believe their ideas and contributions will be respectfully heard and considered (www.ccl.org). Loignon and Wormington (2022) found that teams with higher degrees of psychological safety were more productive and reported lower instances of interpersonal conflicts. It is vital that leaders create a psychologically safe space for employees to offer these diverse ideas because if the workforces do not believe they can trust the leaders or the process, they will not share their ideas or engage in the brainstorming practice. As a result, leaders may make unilateral decisions that only exacerbate the conflicts, which could cause the problem to fester, grow, and eventually spiral out of control (Wilkin, 2023).

Edmondson and Mortenson (2021) offer guidance for leaders to begin these conversations and create a culture of psychological safety. The first step to begin the conversation and recognize creative resolutions to conflicts is more effective when everyone feels safe, and they are willing to generate creative ways to resolve the issues. Leaders who are candid, humble, and vulnerable lead by example, and their employees are more willing to share their own concerns and ideas. Sharing ideas may take some time because employees may not feel safe, or they may not trust that what they say will not be used against them in some way (Wilkin, 2022).

Based on over 2 years of research with almost 300 organizational leaders, Loignon and Wormington (2022) offer the following tips for creating a psychologically safe workplace:
– Make psychological safety a priority;
– Show genuine interest in everyone's ideas;
– Demonstrate that mistakes are lessons learned;
– Encourage creative, innovative ideas;
– Realize that conflict can be constructive if managed productivity;
– Advocate for psychological safety for everyone in the organization;
– Promote open, honest, respectful communication;
– Express gratitude.

Leaders who are mindful about their responses to shared information, who model respect for their employees, and who are genuine and honest can begin to build a psychologically safe workplace (Edmonson & Mortenson, 2021).

*H*one a Mindfulness Consciousness

Until recently, mindfulness was viewed as a nebulous or new-age concept that had nothing to do with the workplace (Wilkin, 2022). However, mindfulness is a valuable tool that can help leaders resolve organizational conflicts and make better decisions (Riskin & Wohl, 2015; Yu & Zellmer-Bruhn, 2018). Mindfulness is defined as focusing our attention and bringing our awareness to experiences without judging them or being attached to a specific outcome (Brown, Ryan, & Creswell, 2007). In today's work environment, where busyness, multitasking, and virtual meetings are normal ways of being, it can be difficult for leaders to focus their attention on what is happening at the moment. Consequently, when conflicts arise, it is easy to slip into mindlessness, act on autopilot, and do whatever we have done before to resolve conflicts, even if we know those methods are ineffective (Riskin & Wahl, 2015). Practicing mindfulness gives us more control over conflicts. If we can be fully present in the moment, we may be more compassionate toward others, ourselves, and the situation. As a result, conflicts are less likely to escalate and lead to workplace bullying (Yu & Zellmer-Bruhn, 2018).

*Th*ink About Emotional Responses

Every conflict is connected to some emotion because if we did not care, there would not be any conflict. Emotions are the windows to people's inner core, and they provide leaders with information that words alone do not offer. Becoming more mindful of emotions is one way to listen and learn without any exchange of words (Wilkin, 2022). Goleman's (2005) model of emotional intelligence provides five concepts that help leaders think more about their emotional responses to conflict situations. His model focuses on self-awareness, self-regulation, empathy, motivation, and social skills (Wilkin, 2023).

Self-awareness and self-regulation are at the core of thinking about emotional responses to conflicts. Self-awareness is the ability to understand your own emotions and determine why you feel a certain way. Self-aware leaders acknowledge their emotions but do not make decisions solely based on feelings. Self-regulation, the second component of emotional intelligence, is the ability to monitor your emotions; emotionally intelligent leaders do not allow others to push their hot buttons. In addition, emotionally intelligent leaders are motivated to accomplish goals (Wilkin, 2023).

Empathy is a significant characteristic of emotional intelligence. In fact, Wilkinson (2019) says empathy is the glue that holds society together. Empathy is the channel that connects people and provides a view of the world through the other person's lens (Wilkin, 2020). Empathetic people are open and honest, and as a result, they easily cultivate relationships. Through self-reflection and self-awareness, empathetic people create and live life authentically without being too quick to judge or stereotype others (Wilkin, 2022).

The final concept of Goleman's model (2005), social skills, encompasses the other four concepts. People with good social skills are team players, and they enjoy mentoring others and helping them grow within the organization. They understand that an organization is most successful when people play well together, and communicating and building relationships are key factors in the way they interact with others.

Although the five concepts are presented as linear, they are interconnected. For example, it is challenging to be self-regulated and motivated if you are not self-aware. Likewise, empathy for others is difficult if you are not aware of your own emotions and what triggers them (Wilkinson, 2019). Empathetic people develop and manage good relationships with others, which is also a part of the concept of social skills.

Designing and Implementing a Conflict Management System

Shining a *LIGHT* on the problem of workplace bullying sets the tone for creating an organizational culture that shows workers that the leaders are serious about eliminating the problem. Conflict is a natural occurrence in workplaces, and normal conflict is not positive or negative. Rather, how conflict is dealt with determines if the outcomes are productive or destructive. (Wilkin, 2023).

Some scholars contend that workplace bullying is an extreme type of interpersonal conflict (Wilkin, 2023) that is exacerbated by an organizational culture that places more importance on profits than on valuing and respecting the dignity of all employees (Einarsen, Skogstad, Rørvik, Lande, & Nielsen, 2018). Others caution against classifying workplace bullying as an interpersonal conflict because it tends to normalize the behavior (Keashly & Hollis, 2023). Regardless of the perspective on how to classify workplace bullying, creating a multi-faceted organizational conflict management strategy to deal with the behavior is a step in the right direction of creating a workplace culture that treats all employees with dignity and respect.

In their research, Einarsen, Skogstad, Rørvik, Lande, and Nielsen (2018) propose three strategies to address workplace bullying. They are:
- Educating Leaders and Employees: Providing education about workplace bullying and emphasizing the value of effective conflict management.
- Developing Procedures: Creating fair, effective, and accessible conflict management procedures.
- Providing Conflict Management Training: Offering training in conflict management skills.

These strategies align with Duffy's (2020) holistic approach. In addition to learning about the problem, organizations can also acknowledge it can happen in their organization, take reports seriously, and align their vision to include respecting and valuing all employees. In addition, she maintains that organizations need to provide skills and awareness-based training, develop anti-bullying policies, and restore harmed workers. She adds that efforts to reduce workplace bullying should include a systemic view, or they are doomed for failure. Workplace bullying may occur between or among individuals, but it cannot occur if the system (the organization) does not sanction it, either intentionally or unintentionally.

Informing and educating organizational leaders and employees through awareness and skills-based training will lead the march to a bully-free environment. When organizations build conflict management training programs into their strategic infrastructure, they can gain a competitive advantage over companies that do not provide these skills. In part, this favorable position is a result of less money spent on litigious resolution processes and less time spent defending claims.

Possible Interventions for Managing Workplace Bullying

So often, leaders simply do not know how to handle reports of workplace bullying. As a result, they either do nothing or exacerbate the problem by denying reports from targets. Leaders can address workplace bullying by becoming aware of the concept, by identifying bullying behavior, and by learning skills that counteract its negative affect (Owen and Demb, 2004). In part, the leaders accomplish this by not only changing their own responses to workplace bullying but also by influencing others to reconsider how they communicate and interact with their co-workers. However, Runde and Flanagan (2006) contend that conflict management may be a challenge for organizational leaders because they have not had formal training in this area. Moreover, they deal with a myriad of personalities, emotions, and situations.

One intervention aimed at helping both the targets and the bullies is by providing a facilitated conversation with a professional mediator. In addition, executive coaching may be an option for bullies who either do not understand the negative impact their behaviors have on their targets or who mistakenly believe that if they do not bully their targets, the work will not be completed properly. Finally, an organizational ombudsperson may also help targets work through the process of reporting the bullying behavior and considering intervention options.

Offering Mediation

Mediation is a powerful tool that has numerous benefits for individuals who experience conflicts with one another. First, the process of mediation empowers people to focus on the problem, not the person, to uncover people's underlying motivations, to discuss their differences, and to resolve the issues that are the root of the conflict situation. Second, mediation deals with human interactions by providing a safe process that encourages open, honest, and respectful dialogue. It is a first step to repairing or improving relationships damaged by conflicts. Perceptions are clarified, and people have an opportunity to open their minds and hearts to see how the world looks through others' lenses. Finally, disputants are more likely to feel that the outcomes are fair, and justice has been served when their voices are heard. Although mediation provides an opening for people to discuss past damaging behaviors, it focuses on the future (Wilkin, 2017).

By facilitating constructive dialogue, skilled mediators can help targets express and defuse negative emotions. Storytelling is a foundation of mediation, and when parties listen to one another, they may become more empathetic to how others feel. In part, understanding the motivations behind bullying behavior can address it. Moreover, through listening to understand, instead of listening to respond, mediation has the potential to empower targets to claim control of their situations and their lives, and to recognize why the bully perpetuates the destructive behaviors. Mediation provides an opportunity for the bully and the target to listen, validate, and address the bullying behavior (Wilkin, 2017). When experiences are validated through listening to concerns, individuals are more likely to feel the outcomes are fair and justice has been served (Barry & Shapiro, 2000; DeKremer & Sedikides, 2008).

Mediation helps people uncover commonalities by encouraging open, honest, respectful dialogue and building trust (Seagriff, 2010). Mediators may empower targets to release negative emotions and help them change their reaction to mistreatment. Cloke and Goldsmith (2000) state that "in mediation, anger is the map to the source of conflict" (p. 67), and mediation helps people acknowledge, uncover, and work through their anger. As a result, they may decide to forgive. Promoting forgiveness through mediation is underutilized because it is viewed as an irrational moral issue that does not result in monetary damages. However, because it deals with the reality of human interactions, it can help amicably resolve disputes involving workplace bullying (Wilkin, 2017).

Through constructive dialogue, effective listening, and establishing a safe environment, mediators can help uncover mutual interests that move the bully, target, and leaders away from anger and blame toward psychological closure. Mediators can utilize their communication skills and intuitive abilities to help the parties let go of the blame and anger. Additionally, the process helps the parties mend, redefine, or end their relationships, while they maintain their emotional balance, selfesteem, and dignity (Moore, 2003).

Some scholars advise against mediation because of the likely power differential between the bully and the target. In addition, the target may be too intimidated to participate in the mediation process (Keashly & Hollis, 2023). In addition, as mentioned earlier, workplace bullying is a conflict that has escalated. As a result, mediation should not be forced on targets; it should be a voluntary intervention. In addition, the mediator should be an outside neutral, not someone from human resources or an internal mediator. The mediators should be completely neutral and understand the escalating nature and power differentials involved in workplace bullying (Jenkins, 2011).

Coaching

Coaching is a technique that may help the bully modify the behaviors that cause the targets pain. It may be helpful to identify two basic types of bullies. First, Crawshaw (2023) maintains there are "abrasive leaders" who do not fully understand the harm they are causing their targets. This is the type that believes they are simply being tough managers and they believe the work will not get done if they do not cajole, ridicule, and intimidate the others (Castle, 2014). Not being tough could reflect on their competency. Crawshaw (2023) contends that an overwhelming majority of bullies she has coached are afraid of being perceived as incompetent, and they are afraid of failure.

The second type of bully fully understands the damage they are causing and relishes the pain they inflict on the targets. The bully in my first study may have feared being viewed as incompetent, but he also clearly understood and bragged about the damage he did to his targets. The leaders simply did not know what to do when the toxic behaviors were reported, so they either did nothing or fired the target, thus exacerbating the problem.

It is possible that either type of bully could benefit from executive coaching if they are willing to improve their communication and emotional intelligence skills. Also, they need to be open to the benefits of changing their behaviors. Therein lies the key. They must acknowledge their negative behavior and make an effort to shift the way they interact with their targets and others. This approach does not mean giving the bully a free pass. It is also important to note that simply terminating the bully is a band-aid approach that may address the symptom but does little to cure the problem. Crawshaw's research aligns with a study by Georgakopoulous, Kent, and Wilkin (2011) that found providing guidelines, coaching, and rehabilitation may be more productive than ceremoniously firing the bully. This may be especially true if bullying is not viewed from a systematic perspective. In fact, the organization may hire the same person in a different body if they value the individual's attributes and skills.

If your organization is considering coaching to remediate the bully, Cinnie Noble's CINERGY™ Model provides a results-proven clear path forward. It is based on the following stages:

- C = Clarify the goal of the coaching – Intended to determine what needs to be achieved.
- I = Inquire about the situation – Intended to clarify and understand the situation.
- N = Name the elements – Intended to increase self-awareness, consider the other person's perspective, gain a deeper understanding or a different perception.
- E = Explore choices = Intended to explore a possible plan of action to reach a goal, including risks and opportunities.
- R = Reconstruct the situation – Intended to select a plan of action based on desired outcomes and provide feedback.
- G = Ground the challenges – Intended to consider any challenges associated with the plan of action.
- Y = Yes to the commitment – Intended to confirm the next steps, learn about takeaways, and discuss moving forward.

Although there is not a set number of coaching sessions needed, the problem did not occur overnight, and it will take more than one session to go through the model and to resolve it.

In her blog, cinergycoaching.com, Dr. Noble offers suggested questions for the bully to guide the coaching sessions and help with each step of the model. Sample questions are:

- What was the situation with the target?
- What impact has it had on you?
- What impact has it had on the target?
- How would you handle the situation differently?
- What would you like to say to the target?
- What would you like the target to say to you?
- What do you see as a path forward?

Coaching is an intervention that may help bullies understand why they behave in certain ways, how it can be hurtful to the target, and what they can do to make changes. For that to happen, bullies need to take responsibility for their actions and have a desire to transform their behaviors.

Ombudsperson

The function of an ombudsperson is to help people and organizations. In part, they offer a safe space for open, honest, and respectful dialogue where employees can discuss their concerns without fear of retribution or retaliation. The success of any organizational ombudsperson depends on them being independent, remaining impartial, and maintaining the confidentiality of employees who use their services. Part of their responsibility is to be an advocate for the individuals who come to see them. Moreover, they are skilled in a number of interventions, including mediation, conflict management strategies, and informal coaching (Belak & Thoele, 2020).

The nature of the ombudsperson's role assures targets are treated fairly, and they can guide the target to explore alternative ways to get help. Listening, reflecting, reframing, and feedback provide targets with an empathetic listener who will also help them identify their next steps. They educate the target about any policies or resources the organization has to address workplace bullying. Their role not only benefits the targets but also helps organizations identify patterns of behaviors and trends, so leaders can address problems and initiate systemic changes (Katz, Powless, & Hardison, 2023). As with mediation and coaching, an ombudsperson can help address workplace bullying if the targets feel safe, if the bullies are willing to change their behaviors, and if the leaders are willing to invest in this resource.

Creating Policies and Procedures to Address Workplace Bullying

Pervasive bullying happens in organizations that sanction it, either intentionally or unintentionally, as a result of their organizational cultures. Keashly and Hollis (2023) conducted a content analysis of four universities with anti-bullying policies, and they proposed elements of a comprehensive policy, including:
- Create an organizational vision for a healthy, respectful, and productive working and learning environment;
- Communicate the responsibility of all employees to support and promote a dignified working environment;
- Define workplace bullying and explain how it damages the vision;
- Explain the roles and responsibilities of leadership, management, and employees at all levels of the organization;
- Clarify where and to whom to report bullying;

- Provide detailed options and processes for reporting and responding to reports of bullying;
- Provide a timeline for the initial response;
- Include and discuss any informal resolution processes;
- Explain the formal investigation process;
- Report what will happen as part of the review process, including:
  - Members of the review/investigatory committee
  - Provision to separate target and bully
  - Possible consequences if bullying allegations are substantiated
- Include a "no retaliation" provision;
- Review and update the policy every 3 years;
- Provide training at least every 2 years for all employees.

This comprehensive policy provides excellent guidelines for organizations. However, each organization will benefit from involving and collaborating with both the leaders and the employees to assure it fits the organization's needs and addresses issues specific to that firm (Duffy, 2020).

Every employee should have access to the policy. Post it on the company's intranet and include it in the employee handbook. Additionally, it needs to be communicated to every employee at every level in the organization. Schedule training and workshops to discuss the policy and the procedures for dealing with reports of bullying. Provide workshops on civility and how to treat employees respectfully. Finally, surveys are a way to be proactive and assure the policy is working as intended (Daniel, 2024).

The Case for Legislation

A third (external) option is legislation. Currently, in the United States, there is no collective law against being a jerk at work, and current anti-harassment or discrimination laws do not always apply to workplace bullying. Although employers typically abhor additional legislation that mandates how they operate their businesses, it is unfortunate that many organizations will not implement internal controls to prevent workplace bullying. Therefore, legislation may need to be considered. Moreover, there is a growing number of advocates who are proposing to follow the actions of other countries and create legislation against workplace bullying. For example, David Yamada, an attorney and anti-workplace bullying activist, contends that the degree, gravity, and frequency of workplace bullying necessitate changes, and internal controls are either not happening or they are not effective. Yamada crafted the Healthy Workplace Bill (HWB) in 2002, and it has been actively intro-duced in thirty-two states. The goal of the HWB is to prevent and correct abusive work environments. It makes provisions for employer liability, damages to the tar-get, and no retaliation against the targets or other individuals who report work-place bullying (Yamada, 2018).

This bill has not been fully enacted in any state. However, California, Tennes-see, and Utah have taken steps to adopt legislation that addresses pieces of the Healthy Workplace Bill. Most recently, Massachusetts, New York, and West Vir-ginia introduced the bill. Moreover, citizens of Hampshire, Massachusetts, voted to approve a public policy question that declared "workplace psychological ha-rassment to be an occupational health issue" and requires employers of fifty or more employees to have an anti-bullying policy in place (www.bullyinginstitute. org). Likewise, Fulton County, Georgia, passed a more inclusive anti-workplace bullying policy that covers county employees. Its purpose is to provide a work-place where employees are treated with dignity and respect. While that policy fol-lows the HWB, as it uses the same definition of workplace bullying, and bullies may be suspended or terminated, there is not a provision for compensatory dam-ages for targets (Yamada, 2018).

In fact, the United States lags behind other countries when it comes to anti-bullying legislation, as it searches for rational strategies, policymakers may want to model these countries' guidelines. In 1993, Sweden was the first country to establish an anti-bullying ordinance. Later, Australia, France, the United Kingdom, Finland, Italy, and Germany followed suit (Cobb, 2018). In 2002, Quebec, Canada incorpo-rated incremental changes to its Labor Standards Act, which renders psychological harassment illegal (Namie and Namie, 2003). The nomenclature is different from country to country. Some use power harassment, mobbing, or psychological harass-ment. However, the goal is the same in all of the countries, and that is to provide a physically and psychologically safe workplace that is free from any risks that pose a threat to employees' security, well-being, respect, or dignity.

Conclusion

After listening to the targets' stories in both my studies, I found that it is critically important for organizational leaders to listen, validate, and act upon allegations of workplace bullying (Wilkin, 2010). Specifically, organizational leaders can begin to address this problem by implementing policies against it, providing skills and awareness-based conflict management training, and incorporating interven-tions that help restore the targets. By doing this, they may lessen the damaging effects of workplace bullying and create a safe, healthy, and harmonious working environment where employees at all levels of the organization feel psychologically safe and are appreciated and respected. These are also internal controls, so organizations remain in charge of their processes for managing workplace bullying behaviors.

References

Adams, A. (2014). Bullying at work: How to confront and overcome it. Virago.

Agotnes, K. W., Einarsen, S. V., Hetland, J., & Skogstad, A. (2018). The moderating effect of laissez-faire leadership on the relationship between co-worker conflicts and new cases of workplace bullying: A true prospective design. Human Resource Management Journal, 28(4), 555–568.

Ashforth, B. (1999). Petty tyranny in organizations. Human Relations, 47(7), pp. 755–779.

Baillien, E., Camps, J., Van den Broeck, A., Stouten, J., Godderis, L., Sercu, M., & De Witte, H. (2016). An Eye for an Eye Will Make the Whole World Blind: Conflict Escalation into Workplace Bullying and the Role of Distributive Conflict Behavior. Journal of Business Ethics, 137(2), 415–429.

Baron, R.A., Neuman, J.H. (1998). Workplace aggression--the iceberg beneath the tip of workplace violence: Evidence of its forms, frequency, and targets. Public Administration Quarterly, 21(4), 446–464.

Barry, B., & Shapiro, D. (2000). When will grievants desire voice?: A test of situational, motivational, and attributional explanations. International Journal of Conflict Management (1997–2002), 11(2), 106.

Belak, A. & Thoele, C. (2020). What in the world is an ombudsman? In L. Wilkin and T. Belak (Eds.) From discord to harmony: Making your workplace hum (pp. 319–332). Charlotte, SC: Information Age Publishing. Charlotte, NC: Information Age Publishing, Inc.

Bjorkqvist, K., Osterman, K. & Hjelt-Back, M. (1994). Aggression among university employees. Aggressive Behavior, 20, pp. 173–184.

Boulding, K.E. (1990). Three faces of power. Newbury Park, CA: Sage Publications, Inc.

Brown, K. W., Ryan, R. M., & Creswell, J. D. (2007). Mindfulness: Theoretical foundations and evidence for its salutary effects. Psychological Inquiry, 18(4), 211–237.

Brumet, R. (2013). Living originally: Ten practices to transform your life. Unity Village, MO: Unity Books.

Butler, D. S., & Mullis, F. (2001). Forgiveness: A conflict resolution strategy in the workplace. The Journal of Individual Psychology.

Butterworth, E. (2004). Celebrate yourself. Unity Village, MO: Unity Books.

Castle, K. M. (2014). The Workplace Bully: A Grounded Theory Study Exploring Motivational Influences of Bullying Behavior at Work (Order No. 3636399). Available from ProQuest Dissertations & Theses Global. (1615412530).

Chappell, S., Cooper, E., & Trippe, G. (2019). Shadow work for leadership development. Journal of Management Development, 38(5), 326–335.

Cloke, K., & Goldsmith, J. (2000). Resolving conflicts at work: A complete guide for everyone on the job (1st ed.). San Francisco: Jossey Bass.

Cobb, E. P. (2018). Comparing and contrasting workplace bullying and mobbing laws in other countries with the American legal landscape. In M. Duffy and D. Yamada (Eds). Workplace Bullying and mobbing in the United States. Santa Barbara, CA: Praeger.

Crawford, N. (1999). Conundrums and confusion in organizations: The etymology of the word "bully." International Journal of Manpower, 20(1/2).

Crawshaw, L. (2023). Grow your spine & manage abrasive leadership behavior: A guide for those who manage bosses who bully. Executive Insight Press.

Dahl, R. (1986). Power as the control of behavior. In Steven Lukes (Eds.), Power: Reading in social and political theory (pp. 37–58). New York, NY: New York Press.

Daniel, T. (2009). Stop Bullying at Work: Strategies and tools for HR and legal professions. Alexandria, VA: SHRM.

Daniel, T. A. (2024). Toxic Leaders and Tough Bosses: Organizational Guardrails to Keep High Performers on Track. Walter de Gruyter.

https://doi.org/10.1515/9783111332260-010

De Kremer, D., & Sedikides, C. (2008). Reputational implications of procedural fairness for personal and relational self-esteem. Basic and Applied Social Psychology, 30(1), 66–75.

Duffy, M. (2020). Recognizing and responding to workplace bullying and mobbing: Guidelines for business leaders. In L. Wilkin and Y. Pathak (Eds.) The handbook of organizational conflict management (pp. 17–33). De Gruyter.

Dyer, W. W. (2001). Ten secrets for success and inner peace. Carlsbad, CA: Hay House.

Edmonson, A., & Mortenson, M. (2021). What psychological safety looks like in a hybrid workplace. Harvard Business Review Digital Articles, 1–7.

Einarsen, S. (1999). The nature and causes of bullying at work. International Journal of Manpower, 20(1/2).

Einarsen, S., Hoel, H., Zapf, D. and Cooper, C. (2003) The concept of bullying at work. In: Einarsen, S., Hoel, H., Zapf, D. and Cooper, C., Eds., Bullying and Emotional Abuse in the Workplace, Taylor and Francis, London, pp. 3–32.

Einarsen, S., & Mikkelsen, E.M. (2003). Individual effects of exposure to bullying at work. In Stale Einarsen, Helge Hoel, Dieter Zapf & Cary Cooper (Eds.), Bullying and Emotional Abuse in the Workplace: International Perspectives in Research and Practice (pp.127–142).

Einarsen, S., Skogstad, A., Rørvik, E., Lande, Å. B., & Nielsen, M. B. (2018). Climate for conflict management, exposure to workplace bullying and work engagement: a moderated mediation analysis. International Journal of Human Resource Management, 29(3), 549–570.

Enright, R.D. (2001). Forgiveness is a choice: A step-by-step process for resolving anger and restoring hope. Washington, DC: American Psychological Association.

Enright, R. D., & North, J. (1998). Introducing forgiveness. Exploring forgiveness, 3–8.

Garmezy, N. (1991). Resiliency and vulnerability to adverse development outcomes associated with poverty. The American Behavioral Scientist, 34(4).

Georgakopoulos, A., Wilkin, L., & Kent, B. (2011). Workplace bullying: A complex problem in contemporary organizations. International Journal of Business and Social Sciences, 2(3), 1–20.

Fehr, R., & Gelfand, M. J. (2012). The forgiving organization: A multilevel model of forgiveness at work. Academy of Management Review, 37(4), 664–688.

Finlayson, L. https://theartoflivingconsciously.com/

Fraser, P. D. (2022). The Bullied Brain: Heal Your Scars and Restore Your Health. Rowman & Littlefield.

Goleman, D. (2005). Emotional intelligence: Why it can matter more than IQ. New York, NY: Bantam Books.

Hasselbeck, P. (2010). *Heart-centered metaphysics: A deeper look at unity teachings*. Unity Village, MO; Unity Books.

Hoel, H., & Cooper, C. L. (2001). Origins of bullying: Theoretical frameworks for explaining workplace bullying. In Building a culture of respect (pp. 21–38). CRC Press.

Hoel, H., Glasø, L., Hetland, J., Cooper, C. L., & Einarsen, S. (2010). Leadership Styles as Predictors of Self-reported and Observed Workplace Bullying. British Journal of Management, 21(2), 453–468.

Holmgren, M. R. (1993). Forgiveness and the intrinsic value of persons. American Philosophical Quarterly, 30(4), 341–352.

Jampolsky, G. G. (2011). Forgiveness: The greatest healer of all. Simon and Schuster.

Jenkins, M. (2011). Practice note: Is mediation suitable for complaints of workplace bullying? Conflict Resolution Quarterly, 29(1), 25–38.

Katz, N., Powless, N., Hardison, G. (2023). Functions and benefits of an organizational ombuds. In L. Wilkin and Y. Pathak (Eds.) The handbook of organizational conflict management (pp. 269–280). De Gruyter.

Keashly, L. & Hollis, L. (2023). Workplace Bullying: Not Just Another Conflict. In L. Wilkin and Y. Pathak (Eds.) The handbook of organizational conflict management (pp. 291–308). De Gruyter.

Kilmann, R. (2023). Thomas-Kilmann instrument (TKI) and the Kilman organizational conflict instrument (KOCI). In L. Wilkin and Y. Pathak (Eds.) The handbook of organizational conflict management (pp. 39–56). De Gruyter.

King, D., D., Newman, A., & Luthans, F. (2016). Not if, but when we need resilience in the workplace. Journal of organizational behavior, 37(5), 782–786.

LaVan, H, & Martin, W.M. (2008). Bullying in the U.S. workplace: Normative and process-oriented ethical approaches. Journal of Business Ethics, 83, pp. 147–165.

Layton, M. (1998). The long road to forgiveness. Family Therapy Newsletter, (November–December 1998).

Leymann, H. (1996). The content and development of mobbing at work. European Journal of Work and Organizational Psychology, 5(2), 165–184.

Loignon, A., & Wormington, S. (2022). Psychologically Safe for Some, but Not All? https://cclinnovation.org/

Madsen, S. R., Gygi, J., Hammond, S. C., & Plowman, S. F. (2009). Forgiveness as a workplace intervention: The literature and a proposed framework. Journal of Behavioral & Applied Management, 10(2).

Mi, C. (2013, April 12). old-lady-young-woman11. Coach Mi Motivate Inspire https://coachmi.com.au/why-men-dont-listen-and-women-cant-read-maps/old-lady-young-woman11/

Moore, C.W. (2003). The mediation process: Practical strategies for resolving conflict (3rd ed.). San Francisco: Jossey-Bass.

Namie, G., & Namie, R. (2003). The bully at work: What you can do to stop the hurt and reclaim your dignity on the job. Naperville, IL: Sourcebooks.

Newman, K. (2016). Five Science-Backed Strategies to Build Resilience: When the road gets rocky, what do you do? Greater Good Magazine. Berkley, CA.

Noble, C. (2012). Conflict management coaching: The CINERGY™ model. Bookbaby.

Oh, V. K. S., & Sarwar, A. (2022). The study of mindfulness as an intervening factor for enhanced psychological well-being in building the level of resilience. Frontiers in Psychology, 13, 1056834.

Owen, P. S., & Demb, A. (2004). Change dynamics and leadership in technology implementation. The Journal of Higher Education, 75(6), 636–666.

Ponder, C. (1966). The dynamic laws of healing. Marina del Ray, CA: Devorss Publications.

Quine, L. (2003). Workplace bullying, psychological distress and job satisfaction in junior doctors. Cambridge Quarterly of Healthcare Ethics, 12, pp. 91–101.

Rayner, C., & Hoel, H. (1997). A summary of literature relating to workplace bullying. Journal of Community & Applied Social Psychology, 7(7).

Riskin, L.L. & Wahl, R. (2015). Mindfulness in the heat of conflict: Taking STOCK. Harvard Negotiation Law Review, 20, 121–155.

Runde, C., & Flanagan, T. (2006). Becoming a conflict competent leader (2nd ed.). Jossey-Bass.

Salin, D. (2003, Oct). Ways of explaining workplace bullying: A review of enabling, motivating and precipitating structures and processes in the work environment. Human Relations, 56(10).

Seagriff, B. L. (2010). Keep Your Lunch Money: Alleviating Workplace Bullying with Mediation. Ohio State Journal On Dispute Resolution, 25(2), 575–602.

Seligman, M.E., 2011. Building resilience. Harvard business review, 89(4), pp.100–106.

Schwarz, R. (2002). The skilled facilitator: A comprehensive resource for consultants, facilitators, managers, trainers, and coaches. San Francisco: Jossey-Bass.

Skogstad, A., Matthiesen, S.B., Einarsen, S. (2007). Organizational changes: A precursor of bullying at work. International Journal of Organizational Theory and Behavior, 10(1).

Steinhardt, M. & Dolbier, C. (2008). Evaluation of a resilience intervention to enhance coping strategies and protective factors and decrease symptomatology. Journal of American College Health, 56(4), pp. 445–453.

Strandmark, M. & Hallberg, LR.M. (2007). The origin of workplace bullying: Experiences from the perspectives of bully victims in the public service sector. Journal of Nursing Management, 16, pp. 332–341.

Thomas, M. (2005). Bullying among support staff in a higher education institution. Health Education, 105(4), pp. 273–288.

Tehrani, N. (2004). Bullying: A source of chronic post-traumatic stress? British Journal of Guidance & Counseling, 32(3), pp. 357–366.

Wilkin, L. V. (2010). Workplace bullying in academe: A grounded theory study exploring how faculty cope with the experience of being bullied (Order No. 3447190).

Wilkin, L. (2017). Mediation as a tool for resolving workplace conflicts. In The Mediation Handbook (pp. 179–184). Routledge.

Wilkin, L. (2020). From discord to harmony: Five skills for helping your workplace hum. In L. Wilkin and T. Belak (Eds.) From discord to harmony: Making your workplace hum (pp. 319–332). Charlotte, SC: Information Age Publishing. Charlotte, NC: Information Age Publishing, Inc.

Wilkin, L. (2022). From disruption to connection: How mindful conflict management builds bridges during the pandemic and beyond. In S. Malka and R. Tiell (Eds.) Back to a New Normal: In search of stability in an era of pandemic disruption (pp.85–96). Charlotte, SC: Information Age Publishing. Charlotte, NC: Information Age Publishing, Inc.

Wilkin, L. (2023). Shining a light on organizational conflict. In L. Wilkin and Y. Pathak (Eds.) The handbook of organizational conflict management (pp. 3–9). De Gruyter.

Wilkin, L. & Hymes, W. (2020). A workplace bullying perspective: Blending the melodies of ballads (the story) with the classical (the research). In L. Wilkin and T. Belak (Eds.) From discord to harmony: Making your workplace hum (pp. 189–199). Charlotte, SC: Information Age Publishing. Charlotte, NC: Information Age Publishing, Inc.

Wilkinson, I. G. (2019). In praise of empathy: The glue that holds caring communities together in a fractured world. Canadian Journal of Family and Youth, 11(1), 234–291.

Wilmot, W. W. and Hocker, J. L. (2001). Interpersonal conflict (6th ed.). McGraw-Hill.

Woolf, J. (2024). How Pixar fosters a culture of vulnerability at work. Harvard Business Review.

Workplace Bullying Institute (2021). The WBI 2021 U.S. Workplace Bullying Study. https://workplacebullying.org/2021-wbi-survey/

Workplace Bullying Institute (2021). The WBI 2021 U.S. Workplace Bullying Study. https://healthyworkplacebill.org

Worthington, E. L. (1998). Dimensions of forgiveness: Psychological research & theological perspectives. In Laws of life symposia series (Vol. 1). Templeton Foundation Press.

Worthington, E. (2001). Five steps to forgiveness: The art and science of forgiving. New York: Crown.

Yamada, D. (2018). The American legal landscape: Potential redress and liability for workplace bullying and mobbing. In M. Duffy and D. Yamada (Eds). Workplace Bullying and mobbing in the United States. Santa Barbara, CA: Praeger.

Yu, L., & Zellmer-Bruhn, M. (2018). Introducing team mindfulness and considering its safeguard role against conflict transformation and social undermining. Academy of Management Journal, 61(1), 324–347.

Zapf, D. (1999). Organizational, work group related and personal causes of mobbing/bullying at work. International Journal of Manpower, 20(1/2).

Index

https://doi.org/10.1515/9783111332260-011

www.ingramcontent.com/pod-product-compliance
Lightning Source LLC
Chambersburg PA
CBHW071749270326

41928CB00013B/2850